EXTRAORDINARY RECIPES FROM

PHILADELPHIA CHEF'S TABLE

APRIL WHITE

Photography by Jason Varney

THE CITY OF BROTHERLY LOVE

LYONS PRESS

Guilford, Connecticut

An imprint of Rowman & Littlefield

Lyons Press is an imprint of Rowman & Littlefield.

All photography © 2012 by Jason Varney

Distributed by NATIONAL BOOK NETWORK

Library of Congress Cataloging-in-Publication Data

White, April.
  Philadelphia chef's table : extraordinary recipes from the City of Brotherly Love / April White ; food photographs by Jason Varney.
      p. cm.
  Summary: "Celebrating Philadelphia's best restaurants and eateries with recipes and photographs, Philadelphia Chef's Table profiles signature "at home" recipes from more than 50 legendary dining establishments. A keepsake cookbook for tourists and locals alike, the book is a celebration of Philadelphia's unique and exciting food scene"—Provided by publisher.
  ISBN 978-0-7627-7762-4 (hardback)
  1. Restaurants—Pennsylvania—Philadelphia—Guidebooks. 2. Cooking—Pennsylvania—Philadelphia. 3. Philadelphia (Pa.)—Guidebooks. I. Title.
  TX907.3.P42W45 2012
  647.95748'11—dc23
                                                                        2012004580

Printed in the United States of America

Restaurants and chefs often come and go, and menus are ever-changing.
We recommend you call ahead to obtain current information before
visiting any of the establishments in this book.

To my sister.

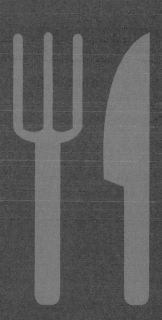

Contents

Entrees 101

Desserts 167

Introduction

Not so long ago, Philadelphia's national culinary identity could be summed up in one predictable word: "cheesesteak." Now, you're more likely to hear food lovers discussing Iron Chef Jose Garces, restaurant mogul Stephen Starr, Marc "Is this the best Italian restaurant in America?" Vetri, and the gelato geniuses of Capogiro than debating the merits of Pat's versus Geno's.

With each bite, the whole country is discovering what Philadelphia diners have known for more than a decade. Beneath the neon and swagger of our signature street food, the City of Cheez Whiz has grown into a bona fide food destination.

There's one thing, though, that hasn't changed from our cheesesteak days, when the rivalries between our colorful cheesesteak vendors earned the humble sandwich its place atop Philly foodie lore. It's still the personalities— the talented chefs, innovative bartenders, and personable owners—that are the driving force behind the city's current restaurant renaissance.

This cookbook is their yearbook—a delicious snapshot of the constantly evolving Philly food scene. It's filled with the cool kids from over fifty of the city's most influential restaurants and bars, the stories behind our top spots, cooking advice gleaned from feeding Philadelphians every single day, and more than seventy of our favorite chefs' and restaurateurs' favorite recipes.

(Go ahead. Ask one of them to sign the yearbook. Stephen Starr just might tell you to "stay cool.")

Yes, you heard me say "restaurant renaissance." Any connoisseur of the Philadelphia food scene knows the term can't be used lightly in this town. It should be said with reverence, definitively, with italics and capital letters—"*THE RESTAURANT RENAISSANCE.*" Because before there could be Garces, Starr, and Vetri, the godfathers of our current restaurant dream scene, there were Steve Poses, Reed Apaghian, and Georges Perrier.

In the 1970s, storied spots like Poses's Frog and The Commissary—we *still* talk about the carrot cake at The Commissary—Apaghian's Astral Plane, and Perrier's Le Bec-Fin reintroduced the restaurant to Philadelphia. This was *The* Restaurant Renaissance, the end of the era of industrial food domination over the city's kitchens and the emergence of quirky, personal storefront restaurants— and equally quirky food personalities—that we now take for granted.

Elaine Tait, then the food critic at the *Philadelphia Inquirer,* captured that moment in her *Best Restaurants Philadelphia & Environs.* (Think of the series as Zagat before the red book took over—and before it was usurped by

Foobooz, Meal Ticket, Grub Street, Eater, and the dozens of other blogs that now catalog Philadelphia's meals on a bite-by-bite basis.)

Of the eighty-six restaurants Tait lists in her 1981 guide—the cover an illustration of identical tuxedoed waiters clutching silver cloches—eleven remain today (though some resemble their former selves in name only). There are a handful of South Philly and Chinatown standards, the indomitable City Tavern, and just a few upstarts like Friday Saturday Sunday. Of Friday Saturday Sunday, which was originally open on those nights only, Tait writes, "That was in the early '70s, when Philadelphians were still being told they didn't go out to dinner."

No one would dare tell Philadelphians that now. All we do is go out to dinner. In recent years it could be argued that food has surpassed everything except cheering—or booing—our sports teams as a citywide pastime.

You could say our second Restaurant Renaissance, the current era of Philadelphia dining, began at six o'clock on August 21, 1998, when big, brash Buddakan opened its doors. (And this being Philadelphia, you know everyone wanted a 7:30 reservation.)

For the city's restaurant scene, which had been adrift since the successes of the 1970s, 1998 was a reawakening. Buddakan, Rouge, and Vetri all opened that year. In many ways the three restaurants couldn't have been more different. Rouge and Vetri were tiny. Both could fit within the confines of Old City's Buddakan, with plenty of room for the eleven-foot gold Buddha. Buddakan and Rouge were personality driven, with showmen Stephen Starr and Neil Stein, respectively, setting the raucous vibe. Vetri's front man was polished, low-key host Jeff Benjamin, while chef Marc Vetri was quietly at work in the kitchen. Vetri and Buddakan reimagined two Philadelphia standards—Italian food that didn't start with South Philly red gravy, and Asian fusion that knew nothing of Chinatown—while Rouge gave us what we knew: a burger.

We loved them all. At Buddakan, we waited in line for wasabi tuna pizza and angry lobster, for the promise of a dinner that was also theater. At Rouge, we hovered for a table on the sidewalk—unheard of before Neil Stein lined up Rouge's thatched bistro chairs—which was nearly synonymous with entree into Rittenhouse Square's exclusive circles. At Vetri we made reservations months in advance for the elaborate tasting menu, willing to trust our dinner entirely to a persuasive young chef.

No timeline is ever tidy, of course: Homage must be paid, too, to Fork, the ideal neighborhood bistro every neighborhood wanted, which opened in Old City in 1997. And to Standard Tap, the city's prototype gastropub, and Audrey Claire, the blockbuster BYOB that gave birth to a new genre, both of which opened in 1999. And, of course, Philly didn't forsake its cheesesteaks—or pretzels or water ice, those other two icons in our holy trinity of street food—in this evolution. Our appetites only grew.

Recently, a local food writer, serving as a celebrity judge at a Philly food truck cook-off, was asked what made the competition's street food vendors uniquely Philadelphian. He paused between bites of fish taco from Guapos Tacos: "They are all in Philadelphia," he said.

Bad joke. Good point. Perhaps the defining theme of this second Restaurant Renaissance is that there isn't one, beyond geography and passion.

In Philadelphia, our city of carefully parsed neighborhood loyalties, geography itself has meaning. This cookbook lists each restaurant's neighborhood before its address, a convenient shorthand for a restaurant's ambition and audience. For the Philadelphia restaurant scene as a whole, in such close proximity to the monolith that is New York dining, definition by geography is particularly revealing: These talented chefs could be in New York. They aren't. They've chosen to live and cook in Philadelphia—often with Philadelphia-made products. With rare exception, the city's top talents are homegrown, and even more rarely do these chefs decamp to other cities. They've learned together, outside the pressure cooker of New York, in the kitchens of Perrier, Stein, Starr, Garces, and Vetri, and then set off to claim their own acre of the fertile Philadelphia restaurant scene to explore their own culinary pursuits.

The miniature Italian kitchen of Vetri alone has served as a launching point for five of the city's favorite restaurants. From here came Chip Roman's tasting menu–focused Mica and Michael Solomonov's modern Israeli Zahav. Here Dionicio Jimenez honed his skills before joining Stephen Starr's funky Mexican restaurant El Rey, and here Jeff Michaud and Brad Spence trained before partnering with Vetri himself to open Italian hot spots Osteria and Amis.

The diversity is delicious, even if the best word anyone can come up with to describe it is a dreaded holdover from 1980s restaurant speak: "eclectic." In defying characterization, Philadelphia may have missed the chance to be Chicago ("cutting edge"), San Francisco ("local"), or Portland ("artisanal"). Our consolation prize is cutting edge *and* local *and* artisanal and a dozen other adjectives.

🍴

By the time you read this, some of the restaurants included here will have closed, the victims of an uncertain restaurant economy or our ever-changing cravings. Some of the chefs may be cooking in new kitchens, as protégés graduate from their mentors and masters experiment with new cuisines. No matter. Large or small, steady or fleeting, universally popular or critically praised—these restaurants and chefs have shaped how we eat.

The recipes and cooking insights the city's chefs have generously provided here ensure that you can always go back for seconds even as the menu of the Philadelphia restaurant scene continues to evolve.

STARTERS & SNACKS

We'll start here: Call them "starters," "snacks," or the outdated "appetizers," Philly diners love small plates. We'll order one or two at the bar before dinner—snacks like Sampan's Beef Lettuce Cups (page 8) and Barbuzzo's Bruschetta with Stracciatella & Fava Beans (page 4)—and another one to share at the start of our meal (maybe Meritage's Mussels in Kaffir Lime Curry Sauce, page 19). At some restaurants, like Mexican small plate Distrito (page 10), you can make a full, fun meal of a collection of dishes that are small in size and big in flavor.

That's why Philly chefs love small plates, too. This is their opportunity to talk diners into something different—Grilled Veal Tongue with Pepper Mostarda (page 30)—and experiment themselves. The best of the city's starters and snacks impress with powerful, surprising flavors, a memorable addition to a restaurant meal or your dinner party.

Barbuzzo

Washington Square West
110 South 13th Street
(215) 546-9300
www.barbuzzo.com

When Barbuzzo, the hotly anticipated third restaurant from 13th Street entrepreneurs Marcie Turney (pictured below) and Valerie Safran, opened in 2010, it began collecting accolades as quickly as reservations. In just the first nine months, Frommer's called the Mediterranean restaurant one of the continent's best new urban restaurants. The James Beard Foundation named it a Best New Restaurant semifinalist. And the *New York Times* took notice, praising the holy trinity of toppings on the *uovo* pizza (brussels sprouts, runny egg, and truffle oil) and the caramel budino, a dessert so popular the restaurant began selling it to go.

Turney and Safran hadn't planned on opening another restaurant. The pair was renovating the space to lease it. "Once we stripped the space, it was beautiful," Turney says. "We had to put a restaurant there."

Barbuzzo is a return to Turney's Mediterranean roots and the first of the couple's restaurants to have a liquor license. That means luscious Italian whipped ricotta, Spanish grilled octopus, Portuguese roasted sardines, and basil lemonade cocktails, inspired by trips through Italy.

"I always knew I wanted to do Mediterranean again. That's the food I really love to cook," Turney says. "And everybody loves Mediterranean."

Whipped Ricotta with Grilled French Table Bread

"This whipped ricotta is by far the easiest recipe ever," says Barbuzzo chef-owner Marcie Turney. "You just put ricotta in a food processor. I didn't know what would happen the first time we tried it, but the texture is amazing, so smooth. We add garnishes depending on the season."

SERVES 4

1 cup sheep's-milk ricotta (cow's-milk ricotta
   can be substituted)
2 tablespoons whole milk
1/8 teaspoon kosher salt
Pinch of black pepper
1/8 teaspoon sea salt
1 tablespoon plus 2 teaspoons extra-virgin
   olive oil, divided
1/2 tablespoon vin cotto
1/8 teaspoon fresh thyme leaves
1/8 teaspoon dried oregano leaves
2 figs, cut into quarters
8 slices 1/2-inch-thick French table bread
   (Barbuzzo uses Metropolitan Bakery)
1/8 teaspoon kosher salt
1/8 teaspoon black pepper

In a food processor, puree the ricotta, milk, and kosher salt until silky smooth, approximately 30 seconds. Spoon onto a serving plate and press a well into the ricotta with the back of a spoon.

Sprinkle pepper and sea salt over ricotta. Drizzle with 1 tablespoon olive oil and vin cotto. Garnish with thyme, oregano, and figs.

To prepare the bread, brush each side with remaining 2 teaspoons olive oil. Sprinkle both sides with salt and pepper. Grill or toast until browned, 30 to 60 seconds on each side.

Bruschetta with Stracciatella & Fava Beans

"This is part of our vegetable board when fava beans are in season," says Barbuzzo chef-owner Marcie Turney. "It's easy and it looks great and it tastes great. When fava beans aren't in season, we make a different type of bruschetta or flatbread."

SERVES 4

2 cups fava beans, removed from pods
1/8 teaspoon kosher salt
Pinch of black pepper
1/8 teaspoon lemon zest
1/2 teaspoon lemon juice
3 tablespoon extra-virgin olive oil, divided
1 tablespoon mint leaves, chiffonade
8 1/2-inch-thick slices French baguette
1 clove garlic
Additional kosher salt and black pepper,
   as needed
3/4 cup buffalo mozzarella, torn into strings
   ("*stracciatella*")
1 tablespoon aged balsamic vinegar

Over high heat, bring a large saucepan of salted water to a boil. Blanch fava beans for 2 minutes. Remove beans and plunge into ice water to stop cooking. Peel and discard tough exterior skin. This should yield 1 cup peeled fava beans. In a small bowl, mash fava beans with a fork. Add 1/8 teaspoon kosher salt, pinch of black pepper, lemon zest and juice, 1 tablespoon olive oil, and mint and fold ingredients together.

Brush baguette slices with 1 tablespoon olive oil and rub cut sides with garlic clove. Season with salt and pepper. Grill or toast until lightly crisped, 15 seconds on each side.

Top each baguette slice with mozzarella and mashed fava beans. Garnish with remaining 1 tablespoon olive oil and balsamic vinegar.

THE INGREDIENTS: METROPOLITAN BAKERY

When Metropolitan Bakery opened its doors in Rittenhouse Square nearly twenty years ago, the shop's artisan European breads were an oddity. "Our first customers thought our breads were burnt!" says owner Wendy Born of the richly caramelized, wild yeast boules and slender baguettes that line the bakery.

Now, those loaves—in country white, whole wheat, organic spelt, and a dozen other combinations—are a city institution and a restaurant go-to. You'll find Metropolitan rolls in restaurants' bread baskets and in their recipes. Chef Marcie Turney uses Metropolitan breads for Barbuzzo's Whipped Ricotta with Grilled French Table Bread (page 3), a simple combination that relies on top-notch ingredients.

As the demand for those "burnt" breads steadily increased, Born and Metropolitan's meticulous baker, James Barrett, expanded the business, opening several more storefronts—always with coffee and a little sample of customer favorites—and an around-the-clock baking facility in Port Richmond, where the loaves are still shaped by hand. The Metropolitan brand has grown, too, to include small sweets (like the delicious, hard-to-find canelle) and cakes, addictive, award-winning granola, and, most recently, a sophisticated take on popcorn, in flavors like stout-almond, bourbon, and spiced peanut butter.

www.metropolitanbakery.com

Sampan

Washington Square West
124 South 13th Street
(215) 732-3501
www.sampanphilly.com

"Chefs have so much more fun cooking appetizers than cooking entrees," admits chef Michael Schulson (pictured below). "Entrees are a commitment. Appetizers are an experiment," he says, offering one explanation for the city's spate of small-plates restaurants. Schulson has two: Izakaya in Atlantic City's Borgata, and Sampan, the stylish-but-affordable modern Asian spot he opened on suddenly trendy 13th Street, extending the city's newest Restaurant Row.

Schulson earned his Asian cooking credentials with stints in well-known Tokyo kitchens and has earned critical raves translating Japanese flavors for his East Coast diners.

Among the small-plate experiments that have earned Sampan and Schulson notice: crab wonton tacos, a Sriracha-spiked Philly cheesesteak on a Chinese bun, his famous edamame dumplings (first created by Schulson for Buddakan, page 84), everything on the popular dim sum brunch menu and, quite unexpectedly, miniature cones of soft-serve ice cream in flavors like Fruity Pebbles and Snickers.

This is a restaurant that likes to surprise. The sleek dining room—sip a mango-cardamom sour and watch the cooks in the open kitchen carefully plate ceviche—doesn't hint at the casual Graffiti Bar tucked into a colorful courtyard behind the restaurant, where scorpion bowls with crazy straws are the drink of choice and Schulson can be found behind the grill. (Or in front of the TV cameras: The chef has been the host of TLC's *Ultimate Cafe Off* and Style Network's *Pantry Raid.*)

"As a chef, I always want to do something fun for my diners," Schulson says.

Sweet Shrimp with Radish & Citrus Salad

"This dish is flavorful yet subtle, combining succulent shrimp with a sweet citrus aioli and earthy radish for texture and balance. Topped with fresh lime segments and baby cilantro leaves, it's bright and fresh but also satisfying," says Sampan chef-owner Michael Schulson. "I love it with a glass of crisp white wine in the summer or a hearty wheat beer in the winter. Take care not to overcook the shrimp, in order to preserve their meaty texture."

SERVES 4–6

For the shrimp:

1 cup mayonnaise
1 lemon, juiced
1 lime, juiced
½ cup sweetened condensed milk
1 teaspoon kosher salt
2 teaspoons granulated sugar
¼ cup grape seed oil
½ cup pineapple juice
4 cups vegetable oil
24 U-15 shrimp, peeled and deveined
2 cups cornstarch
Additional kosher salt, as needed

Special equipment: Thermometer

For the salad:

1 lime, juiced
1 lemon, juiced
1 orange, juiced
½ cup grape seed oil
1 teaspoon honey
Kosher salt and white pepper, as needed
2 limes, segmented, membrane removed
2 stalks celery, thinly sliced
3 radishes, sliced into matchsticks
1 red chile, minced

To prepare the shrimp: Begin by whisking together mayonnaise, lemon juice, and lime juice in a bowl. Whisk in condensed milk, salt, and sugar. While whisking, slowly add grape seed oil and mix well. Continue whisking and slowly add pineapple juice and mix well. Set sauce aside. (Sauce can be made up to 4 days in advance and stored, covered, in the refrigerator.)

In a large heavy-bottomed pot, heat vegetable oil to 350°F. Toss shrimp in cornstarch, shaking off any excess coating. Fry shrimp in batches until golden brown and crispy, 3 to 4 minutes. Remove shrimp from oil with tongs or a metal strainer. Drain on paper towels. Season with salt. Toss shrimp with sauce to coat well.

To prepare the salad: Begin assembling the salad by combining lime, lemon, and orange juices with oil and honey in a bowl. Season with salt and white pepper. Toss lime segments, celery, radishes, and chile with dressing.

To serve: Divide the salad between plates. Top each salad with the shrimp.

Beef Lettuce Cups with Tomato Salad

"When I cook Asian food, I don't want to do what Chinatown does. I think, 'What is a Michael Schulson take on this?'" Sampan chef-owner Michael Schulson says. "I ask, 'What do people think of when they think of a lettuce cup?' Then I deconstruct it. It doesn't look like the lettuce cup you would expect."

SERVES 4

¼ cup sake or dry white wine
½ cup soy sauce
½ cup grape seed oil
12 ounces skirt or flank steak
½ red onion, finely diced
1 tomato, diced
½ Thai red or jalapeño chile, sliced thin
1 clove garlic, chopped
3 basil leaves, chiffonade
¼ cup cilantro leaves, chiffonade
½ cup bean sprouts, chopped
4 tablespoons red wine vinegar
¼ cup extra-virgin olive oil
Kosher salt and white pepper, as needed
1 head Bibb or iceberg lettuce, leaves cut
   in 2-inch circles
½ cup roasted peanuts, chopped

In a large bowl, combine sake or white wine, soy sauce, and grape seed oil. Marinate steak in mixture, refrigerated, for 1 hour.

Light grill or preheat broiler. Remove steak from marinade. (Discard marinade.) Grill or broil steak for 7 minutes on each side (medium rare) to 12 minutes per side (well done). Allow meat to rest for 5 minutes. Slice beef into 1-inch cubes, slicing across the grain.

In a bowl, combine onion, tomato, chile, garlic, basil, cilantro, and bean sprouts. Toss with vinegar and olive oil. Season with salt and white pepper.

Place lettuce rounds on a serving plate. Top each with salad and a piece of meat. Garnish with peanuts.

Distrito

UNIVERSITY CITY
3945 CHESTNUT STREET
(215) 222-1657
WWW.DISTRITORESTAURANT.COM

When chef Jose Garces and his staff traveled to Mexico City to sample the capital's distinctive street food, they booked hotel rooms in Zona Rosa, the city's raucous nightlife district. The garish energy of Zona Rosa—and the flavors they discovered at the hectic, vibrant Mercado de la Merced—was the inspiration for Distrito, Garces's third restaurant.

"*Bienvenidos!*" announces green neon, welcoming diners to the bubblegum pink dining rooms plastered with movie-style marquees advertising south-of-the-border beers and signature margaritas. Over here, Mexican movies, projected on a big screen. Over there, a wall of six hundred *lucha libre* masks. There, diners crowded around a table in a vintage green and white VW Beetle, a nod to Mexico City's ubiquitous taxis. (And behind that door, a purple private karaoke room.)

Garces was also the opening chef at restaurateur Stephen Starr's El Vez. Distrito shares that restaurant's over-the-top Mexican pop culture–inspired decor, but Garces has refined his approach to Mexican flavors. At El Vez, the seven signature guacamoles—"Bazooka Limon" with goat cheese, "Caesar Chavez" with pasilla-balsamic sauce—are prepared tableside on a tricked-out bicycle. At Distrito, a far more traditional guac is served in a sleek silver sphere, with lush crab. Ceviche is topped with lime sorbet, tongue gets the taco treatment, and duck, rabbit, and pork belly star in the mole.

"Mexican food has been a part of my fabric since I grew up in Chicago surrounded by Mexican restaurants," says Garces. "Distrito gives me the freedom to do Mexican food my way."

HUARACHES
ESQUITES Y TAMALES
MOLE POBLANO
CARNE ASADA
QUESADILLAS Y SOPAS
ALAMBRES DE CALLOS
GUACAMOLE Y SALSA
CEVICHES
CAMARONES Y PULPO

Veracruz Ceviche

"You wouldn't see a Veracruz ceviche in Mexican cuisine," says Distrito chef-owner Jose Garces. "We took what is traditionally a stew-y sauce made for red snapper, a very hearty sauce, and turned it into a delicate, chilled sauce with some spice and the brininess of capers and olives for ceviche. It works."

SERVES 4

For the Veracruz sauce (makes 1¼ cups):

¼ Spanish onion, diced
2 garlic cloves, crushed
2 tablespoons extra-virgin olive oil, divided
Kosher salt, as needed
2 beefsteak tomatoes, seeded and diced
1 cup clam juice
½ cup tomato juice
1 bay leaf
1 teaspoon Mexican oregano
2 sprigs thyme
1 tablespoon cinnamon
1 clove
1 teaspoon black peppercorns

Special equipment: Cheesecloth

For the fish:

½ pound red snapper loin
¾ cup prepared Veracruz sauce, divided
4 teaspoons minced green olives
¼ cup diced Roma tomato
4 teaspoons small-diced red onion
1 tablespoon chopped cilantro
1 tablespoon chopped flat-leaf parsley
½ cup extra-virgin olive oil
¼ cup lime juice
Kosher salt, as needed

For serving:

4 teaspoons capers
24 avocado "pearls"
24 sprigs micro oregano

Special equipment: Small melon baller

To prepare the Veracruz sauce: Combine onion, garlic, and 1 tablespoon olive oil in a medium saucepan over medium heat. Season with salt. Sweat until softened but not browned. Add tomato, season with salt, and cook about 15 minutes. Add clam juice and tomato juice and bring to a simmer. Make a sachet of cheesecloth filled with bay leaf, oregano, thyme, cinnamon, clove, and peppercorns. Add to pan and cook for 30 minutes. Remove sachet and discard. Transfer sauce to a blender and puree until very smooth. While the blender is running, add remaining 1 tablespoon olive oil in a slow stream, blending until emulsified. Season with salt. Chill.

To prepare the fish: Using a very sharp knife, slice red snapper into thin slices. Spread 1 tablespoon Veracruz sauce on each of the four plates. Fan fish over the sauce. In a bowl, combine olives, tomato, red onion, cilantro, parsley, olive oil, lime juice, and remaining ½ cup Veracruz sauce. Mix well and season with salt. Spread mixture over fish.

To serve: Garnish dish with capers, avocado pearls created using the melon baller, and micro oregano. Serve immediately.

Fork

OLD CITY
306 MARKET STREET
(215) 625-9425
WWW.FORKRESTAURANT.COM

Since it opened in 1997, Fork has been a Philadelphia fixture, a classy, comfortable Old City bistro with a classy, comfortable menu. Chef Terence Feury, too, is a Philadelphia fixture, known for his time at the elegant seafood destination Striped Bass, as well as stints at The Grill at the Ritz-Carlton and Maia, all now closed.

When Feury became the chef at Fork in 2009, it was a reinvigoration for both.

Fork got a new, well-received seafood-centric menu, reflecting the chef's Mediterranean style and his tastes. And the chef got—finally—a little permission to relax, after years of exacting fine-dining experience.

"The menu seems to be a big reflection of the way I like to eat," Feury says, reading over the midsummer offerings. "Baby artichokes, grilled fava beans, lemon and olive oil, arugula, pistachio and mint pesto, preserved lemon. Fresh, light, straightforward. It's simple and not that simple at the same time.

"The challenge for me was to put my own stamp on the food—and to tailor my style to fit Fork," Feury says. "Here, the style is a little more rustic. There is a freedom in that."

And in that freedom, there are new favorites for the regulars of this old standby—scallops with lemon confit and grilled artichokes, wild salmon with braised lettuce and radishes, and deliciously rustic handmade pappardelle with duck ragu—and the reintroduction of Bistro Wednesday, a no-reservations impromptu dinner party with Feury at Fork:Etc. next door.

ORANGE CORIANDER–CURED WILD SALMON WITH SHAVED FENNEL SALAD

"Curing your own salmon is simple," says Fork chef Terence Feury. "If you are going to a dinner party and you can bring salmon you've cured yourself, everyone is really impressed. You can try different seasonings: coriander and black pepper, or citrus with lemon, lime, and orange zest. Experiment."

(Note: Salmon must be cured for twenty-four hours.)

SERVES 4

¾ pound wild king salmon, with skin
½ cup granulated sugar
¾ cup kosher salt
2 teaspoons ground coriander
1 orange, zested
1 bulb fennel
1 large shallot
6–8 French breakfast radishes

2 lemons, 1 juiced, 1 cut into wedges
¼ cup extra-virgin olive oil
Additional kosher salt and black pepper,
  as needed
8 leaves red-veined sorrel

Special equipment: Mandoline

Place salmon, skin side down, on waxed paper on a small tray. In a small bowl, mix sugar, salt, coriander, and orange zest. Sprinkle generously and evenly over salmon, until about ⅛-inch thick. You will still be able to see the orange of the flesh. Place tray in the refrigerator uncovered, so that air can circulate. Allow to cure for 24 hours. Remove from tray and brush off excess curing mixture. Wrap in plastic and refrigerate until ready to serve.

With a mandoline, shave fennel as thinly as possible and slice shallot and radishes thinly. In a bowl, combine vegetables with lemon juice, olive oil, salt, and pepper. Divide salad between four plates. Thinly slice salmon on the bias. Arrange slices around salad. Serve with red-veined sorrel and lemon wedges.

Baby Artichokes in Olive Oil & White Wine

"Artichokes are a big thing for me. I love them," says Fork chef Terence Feury. "I don't know how many people cook artichokes at home, but everyone should. It's a completely different technique than cooking other vegetables."

SERVES 4

2 tablespoons olive oil
6 cloves garlic
1 medium red onion, sliced thin
1 carrot, sliced thin
1 rib celery, peeled and sliced thin
12–16 baby artichokes or 8 full-size artichokes, trimmed (See "Step by Step," at right)
1 cup dry white wine
2 tablespoons white wine vinegar
2 lemons, cut in half
1 sprig thyme
8 sprigs flat-leaf parsley, divided
1 bay leaf
1 tablespoon kosher salt
Black pepper, as needed

In a large saucepan over medium heat, heat olive oil. Add garlic cloves, onion, carrot, and celery and cook until beginning to brown, about 3 minutes. Add artichokes and cook for 2 minutes. Add white wine and bring to a simmer. When mixture is simmering, add vinegar, lemons, thyme, 6 sprigs parsley, bay leaf, salt, and pepper. If artichokes are not covered in liquid, add water to cover. Place a round of parchment directly on artichokes as they simmer. Cook until artichokes are tender, about 15 minutes for baby artichokes and 25 minutes for full-size artichokes. (Test tenderness by inserting the tip of a knife just above the stem.) If using full-size artichokes, scoop out choke with a spoon. Allow to cool in liquid.

Rewarm over low heat. Serve warm, garnished with remaining parsley leaves.

STEP BY STEP: TRIMMING AN ARTICHOKE

"Artichokes can be intimidating," says Fork chef Terence Feury, "but it is a feather in your cap as a cook to trim them well."

1. CHOOSE

When choosing an artichoke, look for one that is firm and deep green with no discoloration. Test the leaves; they should be crisp, not rubbery, and snap if you bend them back.

2. SNAP

Starting near the stem, snap off the first couple of rows of leaves, working in a circle around the artichoke. Bend each leaf back until it snaps; don't tear them or you will lose some of the edible flesh.

3. TRIM

Continue working your way up from the stem, using a serrated paring knife to trim the remaining dark green leaves until you get to the tender yellow leaves. If trimming a full-size artichoke, cut off the top of the artichoke just above the choke. It is easiest to remove the choke after cooking, when it is easily scooped out with a spoon. With baby artichokes, simply trim the leaves to the top; the choke is edible and doesn't need to be removed.

4. SHAVE

Turn the artichoke so the stem side is up. Using the paring knife, shave the tough outer skin of the stem and any remaining green where you snapped off the leaves to reveal the yellow flesh of the heart.

5. DUNK

Trimmed artichoke hearts will oxidize—or turn brown—quickly. To avoid this, place trimmed artichokes in a bowl with 8 cups cold water and 1 lemon cut in half. The acid helps prevent oxidation.

MERITAGE

GRADUATE HOSPITAL
500 SOUTH 20TH STREET
(215) 985-1922
WWW.MERITAGEPHILADELPHIA.COM

Meritage opened in 2004 as a dimly lit, dramatic ode to big-ticket wines and anachronistic dishes like veal Oscar. This is definitely not that restaurant.

When owners Michele DiPietro and Irene Landy purchased Meritage in 2006, they kept the name, but not the precious concept. They opened the curtains, took off the white tablecloths, expanded the bar, and introduced a more accessible, less expensive New American menu.

No one really noticed—until the Korean fried chicken.

In 2009, DiPietro and Landy installed Susanna Foo alum Anne Coll (pictured below) in the kitchen. Coll brought the Southeast Asian flavors and French technique she knew from the kitchens of Susanna Foo, the produce she sourced from farms near her Lancaster County home, and her playful attitude toward food.

"We need to be affordable, approachable, and fun," says Coll. "We thought Korean fried chicken would be fun."

The Korean fried chicken—the secret is the gochujang chili sauce—was a runaway hit, earning the restaurant attention from the city's food media and its diners, some of whom were surprised to find the restaurant was not the high-priced throwback it had been.

Instead, they found Coll's bright, modern cooking—with many naturally vegetarian and gluten-free options—in a bright, modern restaurant that just happened to be named Meritage.

Mussels in Kaffir Lime Curry Sauce

"I like Southeast Asian food. That's what I eat when I'm not working," says Meritage chef Anne Coll. "Southeast Asian flavors just pop. I wanted to do something a little bit different with mussels and wanted to make a sauce that is gluten-free and vegetarian. Plus we're getting really great Kaffir lime leaves from Green Meadow Farm."

SERVES 4

4 tablespoons olive oil, divided
1 4-ounce package Massaman or other
    yellow curry paste
1 tablespoon yellow curry powder
1 yellow onion, sliced
1 large carrot, cut into 1-inch pieces
1 stalk lemongrass, outer leaves removed and
    remaining stalk sliced thinly
3 cloves garlic, crushed
1 teaspoon grated ginger
2 Kaffir lime leaves (available at Asian markets)
2 13.5-ounce cans Chaokoh or other coconut milk
8 cups water
2 limes, zested and juiced
2 tablespoons fish sauce
2 teaspoons kosher salt
3 pounds mussels, cleaned
2 tablespoons unsalted butter
2 tablespoons chopped cilantro
1 package rice noodles, soaked in water
    and drained
½ cup cherry tomatoes, cut in half

In a large saucepan over medium heat, heat
2 tablespoons olive oil. Add curry paste, curry
powder, onion, carrot, lemongrass, garlic, ginger,
and lime leaves. Cook until vegetables begin to
soften. Add coconut milk and reduce heat to low.
Cook for 5 minutes. Add water and simmer for 45
minutes. Remove lime leaves and puree remaining
mixture in a blender until sauce is smooth. Add lime
zest and juice, fish sauce, and salt.

In a large saucepan over high heat, heat
remaining 2 tablespoons olive oil. Add mussels,
sauce, and butter. Cover pan and cook until
mussels open, 4 to 5 minutes. Add cilantro.

Place rice noodles in a serving bowl. Spoon sauce
and mussels on top. Garnish with tomatoes.

Percy Street Barbecue

South Street
900 South Street
(215) 625-8510
www.percystreet.com

Percy Street Barbecue is not an authentic Texas 'cue joint. There's silverware. There's glassware. There's table service. "But we can still do great Texas barbecue," says chef Erin O'Shea (pictured below), who gets her barbecue cred from ten years of living—and eating—in Texas.

Before opening Percy Street, though, O'Shea took a road trip through Hill Country with owners Michael Solomonov and Steve Cook (who also own Zahav, page 115) and her staff. "Everyone's idea of barbecue is different," says O'Shea. "We took everyone to Texas so we would all be on the same page for what makes great barbecue: meat, salt, pepper, and smoke."

Texas-style barbecue isn't saucy like its Southern cousins, the better to highlight the meat and the smoke from the restaurant's two 2,200-pound, bright red smokers. Still, even with the silverware on the table, the roll of paper towels that arrives with the meal is much appreciated. This is a meal to get into: brisket and baby back ribs by the pound, mac 'n' cheese, coleslaw and collard greens on the side, root beer floats, and red velvet cake for dessert.

"When I see people passing plates back and forth and a big ol' gallon of beer on the table—that is what we wanted to create," O'Shea says.

CHEDDAR-JALAPEÑO CORN BREAD

"I could make up a story about this recipe coming from my grandmother," says Percy Street Barbecue chef Erin O'Shea. "That would be a really romantic story. But my story is romantic from a chef's point of view." O'Shea created this recipe for a wedding that famed chef Daniel Boulud was attending. "I made the recipe so many times, until it was perfect. And after dinner, Daniel Boulud came back to the kitchen. The one thing he talked about was the corn bread."

MAKES 1 LOAF

1¼ cups all-purpose flour
1 cup plus 3 tablespoons yellow cornmeal
3 tablespoons plus 2 teaspoons granulated sugar
1 tablespoon plus 1 teaspoon baking powder
1¼ teaspoons kosher salt
2 large eggs
1 tablespoon light corn syrup
1¼ cups light buttermilk
¾ cup unsalted butter, melted
3 tablespoons pickled jalapeño, diced
3 ounces sharp cheddar cheese,
    cut into ½-inch cubes

Preheat oven to 425°F. Coat a 9-inch square or round pan with nonstick cooking spray.

In a medium bowl, whisk together dry ingredients. In a small bowl, combine eggs, corn syrup, and buttermilk. Whisk to combine. Add buttermilk mixture to dry ingredients and whisk to incorporate. Add butter, whisking to incorporate. Fold jalapeños into batter.

Spoon batter into the pan and place cheese cubes on top. Press cheese into batter, using the back of a spoon to smooth batter as necessary.

Bake until the top of the corn bread is golden brown and a toothpick inserted in the corn bread comes out just a little moist, about 50 minutes. Transfer to rack to cool. Allow to cool at least 30 minutes before slicing.

FISH

WASHINGTON SQUARE WEST
1234 LOCUST STREET
(215) 545-9600
WWW.FISHPHILLY.COM

Chef-owner Mike Stollenwerk made his name at Little Fish, happily shucking oysters to be splashed with sherry mignonette, searing scallops to serve alongside carrot-ginger puree, and slicing the octopus carpaccio that became his signature until the twenty-two-seat BYOB became just too, well, little for the chef's ambitions. So, Stollenwerk's second project was a bigger Fish, with a more upscale vibe and a liquor license, where the chef would have the room to expand his repertoire of creative seafood dishes: crispy skate with truffled spaetzle in a Parmesan broth, swordfish with braised bacon and boiled peanuts, octopus paired with eggplant, cucumber, and lamb.

But at just fifty seats, the second incarnation of Fish was still little by most standards. So, Stollenwerk expanded again, moving the restaurant to Washington Square West. Now the restaurant has nearly one hundred seats—and much more kitchen space.

"We start with the fish," says Stollenwerk, who has a particular fondness for black bass, which has appeared on the Fish menu cooked with butternut squash and brussels sprouts or raw with lemon and basil. "Now that we have the space, we can experiment with ingredients to complement each fish."

"There's still a ton of fish out there I haven't cooked yet," the chef says.

SMOKED SALMON PANZANELLA

"This is a seafood twist on the traditional panzanella," says Fish chef-owner Mike Stollenwerk. "We wanted to incorporate the traditional parts of panzanella and the accoutrements you would usually find with smoked salmon like shallots and boiled eggs."

SERVES 4

½ loaf pumpernickel, cut in 1-inch cubes
6 tablespoons olive oil, divided
Kosher salt and black pepper, as needed
1 tablespoon red wine vinegar
1 tablespoon fresh oregano leaves, chopped
2 large eggs
1 head frisée, torn into pieces
12 ounces smoked salmon, cut in 1-inch pieces
1 pint cherry tomatoes, cut in half
2 small shallots, julienned

Preheat oven to 400°F. In a large bowl, toss pumpernickel with 3 tablespoons olive oil. Season with salt and pepper. Transfer bread to baking pan. Cook until outside of bread is crisp and inside is still soft, about 7 minutes. Return toasted bread to bowl.

In a small bowl, combine remaining 3 tablespoons olive oil, red wine vinegar, and oregano to make dressing. Mix well.

Fill a small saucepan with water and bring to a boil over high heat. Add eggs and cook for 12 minutes. Immediately move pot to sink and run under cold water to cool eggs quickly. Once cool, peel eggs.

Pour dressing over toasted bread and let sit 1 minute. Add frisée, salmon, tomatoes, and shallots. Crumble eggs into bowl. Toss all ingredients to coat well with dressing and divide between four plates.

PHILDELPHIA ICON: PHILLY PRETZELS

Let's set this straight first: The coveted term "Philly pretzel" can't be applied to just any twist consumed within city limits.

We love the big, butter-brushed, pastry-like Pennsylvania Dutch soft pretzels, but those are not the Philly pretzel. And we love hard snack pretzels, consuming twice the national average of crunchy twists, nuggets, rods, matchsticks, and crisps. But none of those are the Philly pretzel either.

As any Philadelphian knows, the true Philly pretzel is a very particular thing: a salt-dotted, double-looped, smooshed oval of a pretzel, crisp on the top and the bottom and chewy on the sides, where it has been torn from a tray of identical twists. The proper Philly pretzel is served with mustard and waxed paper—or a brown box, when you buy by the dozens to share with coworkers or classmates. The best are still warm. We eat them for breakfast—and just about any other time.

It might be fair to say that since the region's German ancestors introduced the Old World creation in the 1700s, there's been only one universally acceptable variation on the original: spontaneous "P"-shaped pretzels when the Phillies win the World Series.

Scallops with Roasted Beets, Pickled Mustard Seed & Pistachios

"This started out as a beet salad," says Fish chef-owner Mike Stollenwerk. "The sweetness of the roasted beets, the heat of the mustard, and the crunch of the pistachios go well together. We were going add goat cheese, but instead we replaced the goat cheese with scallops."

SERVES 4

12 baby red beets
3 tablespoons olive oil, divided
Kosher salt and black pepper, as needed
1 teaspoon sherry vinegar
4 tablespoons cider vinegar
1 teaspoon granulated sugar
½ teaspoon kosher salt
2 tablespoons yellow mustard seeds
2 tablespoons canola oil
8 U-10 dry scallops
2 tablespoons unsalted butter
4 tablespoons toasted crushed pistachios

Preheat oven to 400°F. In a baking pan, toss beets with 1 tablespoon olive oil. Season with salt and pepper. Cover pan with aluminum foil and roast beets until tender, about 40 minutes. Working carefully, remove skin by rubbing beets with a paper towel. Allow to cool.

In a blender, combine 4 peeled beets with sherry vinegar and the remaining 2 tablespoons olive oil. Blend on high for 1 minute until smooth and emulsified. Season with salt and pepper. Set aside.

In a small saucepan over medium-high heat, combine cider vinegar, sugar, and ½ teaspoon salt. Bring mixture to a boil to dissolve sugar and salt. Place mustard seeds in a heatproof bowl. Pour hot vinegar mixture over mustard seeds. Set aside to cool.

In a large sauté pan over high heat, heat canola oil until it begins to smoke. Carefully place scallops in hot oil and sear on one side until golden brown, about 2 minutes. Flip scallops and remove pan from heat. Add butter. Baste scallops in pan with butter for 1 minute. Remove scallops from pan.

Divide beet puree between four plates. Cut remaining beets in quarters, season with salt and pepper, and place on top of puree. Place 2 scallops on each plate and top with pickled mustard seeds. Garnish each plate with 1 tablespoon pistachios.

Amis

WASHINGTON SQUARE WEST
412 SOUTH 13TH STREET
(215) 732-2647
WWW.AMISPHILLY.COM

Cacio e pepe is the simplest of Roman dishes: spaghetti-like *tonnarelli* pasta, tossed with olive oil, black pepper, and pecorino. Apart, the ingredients are staples of an Italian kitchen. Together, they are an inspiration.

For chef Marc Vetri, a taste of *cacio e pepe* in Rome inspired Amis, his homey follow-up to haute-Italian Vetri (page 76) and rustic pizza-and-pasta Osteria (page 108).

It's not as easy as Vetri and his partners—Jeff Benjamin, Jeff Michaud, and Amis chef Brad Spence (all pictured at right)—make it look. It takes talent and time to perfect the alchemy of ingredients—for a classic *cacio e pepe* or a classic trattoria.

The team didn't want to replicate Rome. Instead, Amis is a translation with its broad windows and butcher-block tables, a long bar and an open kitchen. "This is Roman food, cooked in Philadelphia," says Spence, who was previously the sous chef at Vetri. Scouting trips to Rome helped him capture the easygoing attitude and bold flavors of that city: mortadella drizzled with hazelnut honey, grilled veal tongue spiked with pepper mostarda, and meatballs served with tomato-tinged potatoes.

The salumi is all made in-house (including the four-foot-plus, sixty-pound mortadella Spence made for the annual Great Chefs charity event), the offal is a surprising best seller, those meatballs are inspired by South Philly and Vetri's dad Sal—"old school," the menu promises—and the surprising orange-hued potato dish is straight from one of the first meals Spence had in Rome. "We're cooking whatever we're into right now," says Spence.

Grilled Veal Tongue with Pepper Mostarda

"Offal can be a tough sell sometimes," says Amis chef-owner Brad Spence. "When we first put the veal tongue on the menu, we sold just a couple. Then we started sending it out, just putting it in front of them, and they started digging in. It sounds scary, but it tastes a lot like a good hot dog when it comes down to it."

(Note: Veal tongue must be brined overnight.)

SERVES 4

½ cup kosher salt
¾ cup granulated sugar, divided
2 cloves garlic
10 black peppercorns
2 sprigs rosemary, leaves only
6 cups water, divided
1 veal tongue
1 red bell pepper, diced large
1 green bell pepper, diced large
2 tablespoons mustard
8 scallions
2 tablespoons olive oil
Additional kosher salt and black pepper,
    as needed

Special equipment: Grill

In a blender, combine ½ cup salt, ¼ cup sugar, garlic, peppercorns, rosemary, and 4 cups water. Blend for 1 minute to make brine. Transfer to a bowl, place tongue in brine, and refrigerate overnight.

Remove tongue from brine, reserving half of the brine. In a large saucepan over low heat, simmer tongue in reserved brine and remaining 2 cups water for 2 hours. Remove tongue from cooking liquid and allow to cool. Remove skin from tongue and slice into ½-inch-thick slices.

To make mostarda, combine red and green bell peppers with remaining ½ cup sugar in a small saucepan. Cook over low heat until thick and syrupy, about 30 minutes. Allow to cool and stir in mustard.

On a hot grill, grill tongue slices and scallions until nicely charred. Place scallions on serving plate, top with grilled tongue and 1 tablespoon mostarda. (Reserve remaining mostarda for another use.) Sprinkle with olive oil, salt, and pepper.

Bistrot La Minette

Queen Village
623 South 6th Street
(215) 925-8000
www.bistrotlaminette.com

"This is what an authentic bistro looks like," says Philadelphia-born, French-trained chef Peter Woolsey, surveying his first restaurant. Authenticity was Woolsey's mantra when he opened Bistrot La Minette. Yellow walls are painted with wood stain to mimic years of cigarette smoke that the restaurant will never see. Black-and-white images of the French countryside hang above lipstick red banquettes. A carafe of easy-drinking house wine sits on almost every marble table.

This is what a bistro tastes like: *bouchées à la reine aux champignons sauvages* (wild mushrooms in puff pastry), *lapin rôti à la moutarde* (mustard-braised rabbit), and *mille feuille aux framboises* (puff pastry with raspberries). Crisp *gougères,* compliments of the chef, start each meal; house-made chocolates arrive with the check.

And Woolsey's French-born wife, Peggy Baud—who lent her name and recipe for the popular *gratin de pâte* "à la Peggy" (mac and cheese)—teaches the Philadelphia-accented waitstaff the proper pronunciation of these home-style French dishes, so that the bustling restaurant even *sounds* French.

But the sign by the door says it best: *Ici, les vins sont fins et la cuisine soignée.* "Here, the wines are fine and the kitchen cared for."

Oeuf du Pêcheur

"A long time ago, I took a trip up through Normandy, and I had this dish in a little seafood restaurant in Honfleur," says Bistrot La Minette chef-owner Peter Woolsey. "I forgot about it until I came across it in a book. Now it's a staple in the restaurant. It's decadent, without having many of the ingredients that you think of as decadent."

SERVES 4

50 Blue Bay or Prince Edward Island mussels
3 tablespoons unsalted butter, divided
2 cloves garlic, roughly chopped
1 large shallot, sliced
1 cup white wine
2 cups heavy cream
4 slices thick-cut country-style French bread
1 cup white wine vinegar

4 cups water
4 large eggs
¼ cup chopped tarragon
1 large egg yolk
Kosher salt and white pepper, as needed

Special equipment: Thermometer

To prepare the mussels, scrub with a brush to remove any seaweed or grit.

In a large saucepan with a lid, melt 2 tablespoons butter over medium heat. Sweat garlic and shallots in butter until softened but not browned. Add mussels and white wine and cover. Cook mussels until they open, about 5 minutes.

Strain mussels, garlic, and shallots from the broth, reserving mussels and broth. Return broth to saucepan and bring to a boil over high heat. Reduce broth by half. Add cream and reduce broth by half again. Reduce to a simmer. Remove mussels from shells, reserving mussels and 12 shells, for presentation.

Toast bread and spread with remaining 1 tablespoon butter. Keep hot in a warm oven.

In a small saucepan, combine white wine vinegar and water to 180°F to poach eggs. (See "Step by Step," page 69.) Poach until just set, about 4 minutes. Using a slotted spoon, remove eggs from water and place on buttered toast.

Add tarragon to broth. Whisk in egg yolk and continue to simmer to thicken. (Do not boil as broth will curdle.) Season with salt and white pepper. Add reserved mussels. Once heated through, divide between four plates, spooning mussels and broth over each egg and garnishing with mussel shells.

NOBLE: AN AMERICAN COOKERY

That the natural world—seasonality, sustainability—is a driving force behind Noble is evident everywhere, from the salvaged hickory floors to the natural light streaming through skylights and open cafe windows, from the distinctive bar formed from a naturally fallen ancient bubinga tree to the cocktails served up at the bar.

Noble, from restaurateurs Todd Rodgers and Bruno Pouget, isn't content with the trendy farm-to-table concept. Noble also practices farm-to-bar, where talented tender Christian Gaal creates unique cocktails—like the absinthe-grapefruit Honey Badger or the Mellow Time with bourbon, pears, and smoked salt—with syrups and other mixers created in-house from seasonal ingredients.

"Cocktails and food go hand and hand for a complete dining experience," says Rodgers, "and seasonality is important in both."

Gaal's cocktails complement chef Brinn Sinnott's menu of beautifully plated modern American dishes, often created with hyper-local ingredients. Call it rooftop-to-table: Above the Center City restaurant grow herbs and edible flowers, tomatoes and cucumbers, blueberries and strawberries.

"It changes the direction of your thinking," says Sinnott, who creates his modern American menu from his small harvest, instead of planning a menu and then sourcing the ingredients. The rooftop ingredients find their way onto Noble's menu as accents and garnishes—and one night a month in growing season, the chef hosts a special dinner using only produce from the sky-high garden.

NOBLE: AN AMERICAN COOKERY [2009–2011]

Unfortunately Noble closed its doors in 2011.

WHY WE'LL MISS IT: "We wanted to focus equally on the quality of the food and the drinks," says Noble owner Todd Rodgers. "The wine, beer, and cocktail list should change as frequently as the dinner menu does."

WHY IT CLOSED: "This was the worst economy in our lifetimes," says Rodgers. "We were really doing what we set out to do, but closing made the most sense to us and our families."

WHAT COMES NEXT: Stephen Starr has turned the Sansom Street space into Italian Il Pittore.

Grilled Rock Octopus
with Zucchini & Garden Herbs

"This was more or less a spontaneous dish, based on what was available in the garden at that moment," says Noble: An American Cookery chef Brinn Sinnott. "I knew I wanted to incorporate basil and lemon verbena. I tried to find a recipe that would highlight those flavors and aromas. All the techniques here are pretty easy. You just need to buy—or grow—the best ingredients."

SERVES 4

For the octopus spice mix (makes ¼ cup):

2 tablespoons black peppercorns
1 tablespoon coriander seeds
1 teaspoon fennel seeds
5 cloves
1 teaspoon cumin seeds
½ cinnamon stick
1 teaspoon ground nutmeg
½ teaspoon ground turmeric
½ teaspoon ground ginger
2 teaspoons mild smoked paprika

For the zucchini puree (makes 1 cup):

2 pounds small zucchini
½ cup plus 2 tablespoons extra-virgin
   olive oil, divided
1 Spanish onion, thinly sliced
5 cloves garlic, thinly sliced
1 teaspoon kosher salt
1 cup water
1 cup mixed herb leaves (such as basil
   and lemon verbena)

For the rock octopus:

4 quarts water
½ cup plus 1 teaspoon kosher salt, divided
1 cup red wine vinegar
4 small Spanish rock octopus
1 teaspoon coriander seeds
1 teaspoon fennel seeds
1 teaspoon black peppercorns
1 teaspoon cumin seeds
4 star anise
12 cloves garlic, divided
1 sprig thyme, plus 2 tablespoons fresh
   thyme leaves, divided
1 lemon, juiced and zested
2 tablespoons prepared octopus spice mix
1 cup extra-virgin olive oil

Special equipment: Cheesecloth

For serving:

4 padron peppers
¼ cup extra-virgin olive oil
4 slices serrano ham
1 cup mixed herb leaves (such as basil
   and lemon verbena)

Special equipment: Grill

To prepare the spice mix: Bring a dry sauté pan to medium-high heat and toast the peppercorns, coriander, fennel seeds, cloves, cumin, and cinnamon until fragrant and slightly smoking. Remove from pan and cool to room temperature. Grind spices into a powder using a coffee grinder. Add remaining spices and pulse to combine. Store in a sealed jar for up to 3 weeks.

To prepare the zucchini puree: Peel zucchini skin with a peeler into thin strips. Slice zucchini into thin rounds. In a sauté pan over medium-high heat, fry zucchini skin in 2 tablespoons olive oil until bright green, about 1 minute. Immediately drain skins on paper towels and refrigerate. Reduce heat to medium and cook onion and garlic in remaining ½ cup olive oil until soft and golden, but not caramelized. Add zucchini slices, salt, and water and cook, partially covered, until zucchini is soft and water has evaporated. Refrigerate until chilled. In a blender, combine zucchini skin and zucchini and puree until smooth. Add herbs and puree again. Refrigerate until ready to use.

To prepare the octopus: In a large saucepan over high heat, bring water, ½ cup salt, and vinegar to a boil. Wash octopus in cold water. Remove head and beak, and cut each octopus in half. In a dry sauté pan over medium-high heat, toast coriander, fennel seeds, peppercorns, cumin, and star anise until fragrant and slightly smoking. With cheesecloth, make a sachet of toasted spices, 4 cloves garlic, and 1 thyme sprig. Add sachet and octopus to boiling water. Reduce heat and simmer until octopus is tender, but not mushy, about 1 hour. Drain and allow octopus to cool to room temperature.

Grate remaining 8 cloves garlic. In a medium heat-proof bowl, combine grated garlic, lemon juice and zest, remaining 2 tablespoons thyme leaves, octopus spice mix, and remaining 1 teaspoon salt. Mix well. In a small saucepan over medium-high heat, heat olive oil until hot but not smoking. Pour

hot oil over spice mixture and mix. Add cooled octopus and toss to coat. Marinate for 1 hour.

To serve: Over medium-high heat, grill peppers until skin blisters. Remove skin and gently rinse peppers. Remove core and seeds and slice peppers into strips. Over medium-high heat, grill marinated octopus until lightly charred and heated through. Slice octopus into individual tentacles. In a medium bowl, toss octopus with peppers and olive oil.

Place 1 tablespoon of prepared zucchini puree in the center of each plate. Divide octopus between plates. Cover octopus with a slice of serrano ham. Sprinkle ham with mixed herbs.

Perfect Pairing

THE SEARCHERS COCKTAIL
{NOBLE: AN AMERICAN COOKERY}

"This started as a conversation with a couple of customers who were visiting from Austin, Texas," says bartender Christian Gaal. "I had heard about micheladas, beer with tomato juice, but they told me about cheladas, beer with savory and spicy elements but no tomato juice. The spiciness doesn't assert itself until the end. The finish is what intrigues you and makes you want to take another sip."

(Note: Oleo-saccharum must be made in advance and the syrup gets spicier the longer it is stored.)

SERVES 1

For the hot pepper oleo-saccharum
  (makes ½ quart):

3 jalapeños, sliced
1 cup granulated sugar
1 cup water

For the cocktail:

1½ ounces blanco tequila
1 ounce lemon juice
1 ounce hot pepper oleo-saccharum
Ice
6 ounces hoppy pale ale or IPA
Lemon wheels

Special equipment: Cocktail shaker

To prepare the hot pepper oleo-saccharum: In a small saucepan, muddle peppers with sugar until well distributed. Let stand until sugar is moist and green with pepper oils, about 10 hours. Add water and bring to a boil over medium heat, stirring occasionally. Strain and cool.

To prepare the cocktail: Combine tequila, lemon juice, and oleo-saccharum with ice in a cocktail shaker. Shake briefly and strain into a pilsner glass. Fill to three-quarters full with beer. Add ice to fill glass. Stir briefly. Garnish with lemon wheels.

Alma de Cuba

Rittenhouse Square
1623 Walnut Street
(215) 988-1799
www.almadecubarestaurant.com

The idea for a Latin restaurant had been on Stephen Starr's mind for a long time. Latin, in fact, had been the original concept for the space that became Buddakan (page 84).

"I was going to Miami a lot in the late '80s and early '90s," Starr says. "I was in love with all the little Cuban places, classic places like Versailles, and modern places like Yuca."

Versailles is as close to Cuba as most can legally go, a four-decade-old Little Havana landmark known for its homey pre-Castro cooking. Yuca—an acronym for Young Urban Cuban-Americans—is the next generation of that Cuban cuisine. Yuca, which opened in 1989, and its superstar chef, Douglas Rodriguez, invented the term "Nuevo Latino cuisine."

Starr partnered with Rodriguez to create Alma de Cuba, bringing his sexy style of Cuban food and cocktails like the passion fruit Alma Colada—and not incidentally, Rodriguez protégé Jose Garces, who would go on to open Amada (page 120) and numerous other Philadelphia hot spots—to Walnut Street.

The dimly lit restaurant, illuminated by portraits and landscapes from its namesake island, dresses up the classic flavors of Cuba—chorizo is sandwiched in a slider with classic Cubano additions pickle and mustard; fried oysters top fufu, the traditional mashed plantain dish; and recognizable sour orange mojo sauce shares the menu with a unique maple version. For dessert: chocolate-dusted almond cake "cigars," with a gold-foil Alma de Cuba cigar band and a book of sugar matches.

Empanada de Verde with Onion Confit & Artichoke Escabeche

"We wanted to make something vegetarian that would be exciting and appeal to everyone," says Alma de Cuba chef Douglas Rodriguez. "Usually, when you see a vegetarian dish, it consists of the same usual suspects of ingredients, like mushrooms since they're meaty. We wanted to do something different, and this dish actually incorporates vegetables in both the crust and filling."

SERVES 4

For the onion confit:

1 yellow onion, diced
1 sprig rosemary, leaves only
1 teaspoon red pepper flakes
2 cloves garlic
½ cup extra-virgin olive oil
Kosher salt and black pepper, as needed

For the artichoke escabeche:

2 tablespoons olive oil
4 artichokes, trimmed and hearts sliced
    very thinly (See "Step by Step," page 17)
¼ cup apple cider vinegar
2 tablespoons honey
1 tablespoon flat-leaf parsley, chopped
1 piquillo pepper, julienned
1 lemon, juiced and zested

For the empanadas:

2 green plantains, peeled and cut into 1-inch
   pieces

2 teaspoons kosher salt

¼ pound yucca, diced small

2 cups whole milk

Additional kosher salt and black pepper, as needed

2½ pounds baby spinach

2 tablespoons olive oil

2 cloves garlic, chopped

1 yellow onion, diced small

8 ounces manchego cheese, grated

8 cups canola oil

Special equipment: Food mill or ricer, thermometer

To prepare the onion confit: In a small saucepan over medium heat, combine all ingredients for the onion confit mixture and season with salt and pepper. Simmer until everything has softened, about 30 minutes. Place mixture in a blender and blend until smooth. Refrigerate until ready to use.

To prepare the artichoke escabeche: Heat olive oil in a sauté pan over medium heat. Sauté artichokes until soft, 3 to 4 minutes. Add vinegar and honey to deglaze the pan, cooking until almost dry. Remove pan from heat and add parsley, pepper, and lemon juice and zest. Refrigerate until ready to use.

To prepare the empanadas: Place plantains in a medium saucepan. Add water to cover and season with 2 teaspoons salt. Boil over high heat until plantains are very soft, about 1 hour. Remove plantains and process with a food mill or ricer. Allow dough to cool slightly and shape into 8 balls. Place each ball between two sheets of plastic wrap and use a rolling pin to roll dough to about ¼-inch thick. Refrigerate until ready to use.

In a medium saucepan over low heat, combine yucca and milk. Simmer until yucca is tender, about 1 hour. Place mixture in a blender and blend until smooth. The mixture will thicken like a light cream sauce. Set aside.

Fill a large saucepan with water, season with salt, and bring to a boil over high heat. Add spinach and blanch until wilted, about 1 minute. Remove spinach and plunge into ice water to stop cooking. Once cool, remove spinach and squeeze out remaining water. Place in a mixing bowl.

In a medium sauté pan over medium heat, heat olive oil and sweat garlic and onion until softened but not browned. Add onion mixture to mixing bowl with spinach.

Slowly add yucca mixture to spinach-onion mixture, stirring until it resembles creamed spinach. (You may not use all the yucca mixture.) Add cheese and season with salt and pepper. Refrigerate until ready to use.

To make empanadas, divide spinach filling between plantain rounds, mounding filling in the center of the dough. Fold dough in half and crimp the edges with a fork. Refrigerate for 3 hours to set.

In a large, heavy-bottomed pan, heat oil to 350°F. Place 1 or 2 empanadas at a time into the oil and fry until deep golden brown and crispy. Remove from oil and season with salt.

To serve: Divide escabeche and onion confit between four plates and top with empanadas.

The Farm and Fisherman

Washington Square West
1120 Pine Street
(267) 687-1555
www.thefarmandfisherman.com

There is no shortage of Philadelphia restaurants that claim the "farm-to-table" title, proudly listing the names of the region's rock star farmers on their menus. Then there's The Farm and Fisherman, from chef-owner Joshua Lawler. Lawler, who earned his local food cred at Blue Hill at Stone Barns, the well-respected New York restaurant with its own eighty-acre farm, has moved past farm-to-table. Using the best ingredients from thoughtful local producers is a given. Raising those ingredients to another level in the kitchen is the next challenge.

The Farm and Fisherman was a homecoming for Lawler and his wife and partner, Colleen, who is also a chef (both pictured below). Lawler learned to cook here, alongside his grandfather, a butcher. He farmed in his Conshohocken backyard and fished at the Shore, where he now sources the seafood for the restaurant.

The ingredients Lawler discovers at the area's farmers' markets—"I can't sit down and just imagine dishes in my head, like a lot of chefs can. I need to go and see the product and meet the people," Lawler says—are transformed in his tiny kitchen into beet "steak" with balsamic glaze, sashimi in rhubarb broth, and roasted lamb loin with farmer's cheese spaetzle. In search of the perfect egg, Lawler contracted with a New Jersey farmer to raise free-range laying hens. "You can really taste the difference," the chef says.

BLUEFISH CONFIT

"I grew up fishing in Cape May," says The Farm and Fisherman chef-owner Joshua Lawler. "We always caught lots of bluefish and didn't know what to do with them. Bluefish had the reputation of being an oily fish, and everyone wanted flounder. In this recipe, you poach the bluefish gently and it doesn't get pungent or fishy."

SERVES 4

1½ pounds bluefish fillets, pin bones
    and skin removed
Kosher salt, as needed
4 cups plus 2 tablespoons extra-virgin
    olive oil, divided
4 cloves garlic, smashed
4 sprigs lemon thyme
1 fresh bay leaf
3 cups diced mixed potatoes
1 tablespoon kosher salt
½ cup diced celery
1 tablespoon coriander seeds, lightly toasted
    and cracked in a mortar and pestle
1 tablespoon sherry vinegar
3 tablespoons lemon juice
Sea salt and white pepper, as needed
1 tablespoon chopped chives
2 tablespoons celery leaves
¼ cup miniature greens
4 slices grilled whole grain bread
1 cup plain yogurt, hung in cheesecloth
    overnight to remove water

Special equipment: **Cheesecloth**

Preheat oven to 160°F. Season bluefish with salt and allow to rest in refrigerator for 10 minutes. Transfer to baking pan and cover with 4 cups olive oil. Add garlic, thyme, and bay leaf. Cover pan with aluminum foil. Cook until fish flakes apart easily but is still translucent, about 90 minutes. Remove from oven and let rest in oil until ready to serve.

Place potatoes in a small saucepan and cover with water. Add 1 tablespoon kosher salt. Over medium heat, slowly bring water to a boil. When water begins to boil, remove from heat and allow potatoes to rest in water. Fill a separate small saucepan with water. Salt generously and bring to a boil over high heat. Cook diced celery for 20 seconds and transfer to an ice bath to halt cooking. Celery should still have a nice crunch. Strain potatoes and celery. In a bowl, combine potatoes, diced celery, coriander, sherry vinegar, lemon juice, and remaining 2 tablespoons olive oil. Season with salt and white pepper. Serve at room temperature.

Divide potato salad between four plates. Carefully remove bluefish from oil. Remove any dark meat or blood line and cut into 1-inch pieces. Place fish on top of potato salad. Garnish with sea salt, chives, celery leaves, and miniature greens. Serve with grilled bread spread with yogurt.

Soups & Salads

It's a predictable question: "Soup or salad?" The answer, in Philadelphia, is both—with the promise that nothing about the city's best soups and salads is predictable.

Peruse the menu and it's quickly clear that our chefs' inspirations aren't iceberg lettuce and chicken noodle.

At Supper, marshmallow tops the Carrot & Orange Soup (page 48). At MidAtlantic Restaurant & Tap Room, angel food cake stands in for croutons on the Roasted Beet Jar salad (page 63). Hearts of palm get the classic French stew treatment at Vedge (page 51), bacon and eggs star in the traditional central France Salade Lyonnaise at Parc (page 66), and watermelon is treated as a green as the central component of Kanella's savory feta and almond-topped salad (page 72).

Remember: These flavorful dishes don't have to be considered sides. On a warm summer day, Tria's Grilled Asparagus Salad (page 70) and a glass of wine is all you need.

Supper

SOUTH STREET
926 SOUTH STREET
(215) 592-8180
WWW.SUPPERPHILLY.COM

Supper chef-owner Mitch Prensky (pictured below) has a habit of being just ahead of the trends. Prensky, who also owns The Global Dish Caterers with his wife, Jennifer, ran a series of pop-up restaurants before the term was even coined. (Prensky called them "restaurant raves.") Then, just as farm-to-table one-upmanship gripped Philly, Prensky contracted with a seventy-five-acre farm in Delaware County to grow produce exclusively for the restaurant.

So it is a surprise to find that despite the small plates and seasonal, chef-harvested menu, nothing about Prensky's cooking or his affable Supper restaurant screams trendy.

As the folksy name implies, the restaurant has a casual, kiss-the-chef vibe—and people do. Prensky is well known to his customers, from his catering days, his open kitchen, and his habit of working the dining room—an eclectic mix of bold art and quirky eBay finds—in his chef's whites.

Those of-the-moment small plates? Prensky likes them because "you can be bolder with flavor combinations." And the ubiquitous "farm-to-table" description? "There are a lot of people jumping on the trend. Everything's 'farm-to-table,'" Prensky says. "We're trying to shorten the distance between the farm and the table."

On the table are dishes as meticulous and carefully composed as the restaurant is comfortable: deviled eggs of the day (think wasabi and nori, saffron and salt cod, Sriracha and pickled daikon, or bacon and cheddar), carrot and orange soup garnished with marshmallows, duck confit on pecan-sage waffles, or the Daily Harvest, a three-course vegetarian menu straight from the farm.

Carrot & Orange Soup with Coconut Marshmallow

"What I love about this soup is the marshmallow," says Supper chef-owner Mitch Prensky. "It gives it an almost creamy base. It speaks to my theory and style of creating a dish: balancing different flavors on your palate at the same time. And you can make the soup ahead of time and then just whip up the marshmallow in two minutes."

SERVES 4

For the soup:

2 tablespoons unsalted butter
6 large carrots, sliced
3 shallots, sliced
Kosher salt and white pepper, as needed
4 cups fresh orange juice
2 cups water
1 sprig thyme

For the coconut marshmallow:

5 egg whites, at room temperature
¼ teaspoon cream of tartar
¼ cup coconut powder (available at Asian markets)
1 cup superfine sugar
1/3 cup water

Special equipment: Thermometer, pastry brush

For serving:

8 fresh mint leaves, torn
1 orange, zested and segmented

Special equipment: Pastry bag, crème brûlée torch

To prepare the soup: In a large saucepan over medium heat, melt butter. When butter is melted, add carrots and shallots. Season with salt and white pepper. Cover saucepan, turn heat to low, and sweat vegetables, stirring often, until softened but not browned, about 20 minutes.

Remove cover and add orange juice, water, and thyme sprig. Increase heat to high and bring to a boil. Reduce heat to low and simmer for 30 minutes. Remove thyme sprig. Transfer soup to blender and puree. Season with salt.

To prepare the coconut marshmallow: In the bowl of an electric mixer, whip egg whites on low speed until foamy. Add cream of tartar and increase speed to medium. Continue to beat until soft peaks form. Add coconut powder and mix until incorporated.

In a small saucepan over low heat, combine sugar and water. Swirl the pot over the burner to dissolve the sugar completely. Do not stir. Increase heat to medium-high and boil to soft-ball stage (235–240°F). Use a thermometer for accuracy. With a wet pastry brush, wash down the inside walls of the saucepan to prevent sugar crystals from forming around the sides.

With the electric mixer running, pour the hot sugar syrup in a thin stream over the fluffed egg whites. Beat until egg whites are stiff and glossy.

To serve: Transfer marshmallow to pastry bag and pipe marshmallow into each of four deep-sided serving bowls. With a spoon, smear the marshmallow inside each bowl. With a crème brûlée torch, lightly toast the marshmallow. Divide soup between bowls and garnish with mint, orange zest, and orange segments.

VEDGE

WASHINGTON SQUARE WEST
1221 LOCUST STREET
(215) 320-7500
WWW.VEDGERESTAURANT.COM

"This is a vegetable moment," says Vedge chef-owner Rich Landau, surveying the nation's dining scene. Landau was well ahead of the trend. He has been cooking gourmet vegan food in Philadelphia for seventeen years, first at vegan Horizons in Willow Grove, then at the restaurant's reincarnation near South Street, which he closed in 2011. Now there's Vedge, a vegetable-focused vegan destination in Washington Square West. "There's a lot of people out there who would come to a 'vegetable restaurant' but wouldn't come to a 'vegan restaurant,'" Landau says. (Horizons devotees: Don't worry. The restaurant's famous grilled seitan is still on the menu.)

Housed in the former Deux Cheminees, Vedge is a sexier, more sophisticated version of Horizons, with both small plates—a vegetable bar will plate "vegetable charcuterie," like Landau's portobello carpaccio—and larger vegetable-centric entrees.

The inspiration for Vedge was Los Angeles's "meat-meat-meat" Animal. "We really want to be that vegetable counterpart," Landau told the Philly food media when the restaurant opened, "which is ironic, because they're in L.A. and we're here in Philly, and it really should be the other way around."

A seitan chef in a cheesesteak town, Landau is constantly challenged to convince diners that vegetables are as satisfying a meal as meat. He's his own toughest audience. "I became a vegetarian when I was a teenager for ethical reasons," he says. "But I was already a carnivore. My palate already knew those flavors. I turn vegetables and proteins like tofu into great meals so that I don't crave meat."

HEARTS OF PALM, BEACH STYLE

"This funky recipe is my take on a beachside soup that you might find in France or the French Caribbean, using hearts of palm instead of fish," says Vedge chef-owner Rich Landau. "It's a pretty cool recipe: easy, with amazing results."

SERVES 4

4 tablespoons olive oil, divided
1 cup chopped leeks
1 clove garlic, minced
¼ cup white wine
8 cups vegetable stock
2 cups diced Yukon Gold potatoes
1 tablespoon Old Bay or other seafood seasoning
1 teaspoon fennel seeds
Sea salt and black pepper, as needed
2 cups diced plum tomatoes
2 16-ounce cans hearts of palm, drained, rinsed, and cut into 1-inch pieces (2 12-ounce packages of fresh hearts of palm can be substituted)
½ teaspoon saffron threads
1 tablespoon chopped tarragon leaves
1 baguette, cut into 1-inch slices and toasted

In a saucepan over medium-high heat, heat 2 tablespoons olive oil. Add leeks and garlic and sauté until fragrant, 3 to 5 minutes.

Add wine. Reduce heat and simmer until reduced by half.

Add vegetable stock, potatoes, seafood seasoning, and fennel seeds. Season lightly with salt and pepper, and simmer until potatoes are almost cooked, about 8 minutes. Add tomatoes, hearts of palm, and saffron. Cover and simmer until potatoes are fully cooked, 5 to 10 minutes.

Stir in tarragon and remaining 2 tablespoons olive oil. Season with salt and pepper again. Divide between four bowls and serve with toasted baguette slices.

Chilled Cucumber-Avocado Soup with Smoked Pumpkin Seeds

"This soup is inspired by one I ate in Nicaragua," said Vedge chef-owner Rich Landau. "The minute I tasted it, I said, 'This is on the menu the minute we get back.' The key to the soup is the texture of the cucumber. It's like shaved ice. That's the food processor. If you made this with a blender, it would be a watery mess."

SERVES 4

For the soup:

4 cucumbers, peeled, seeded, and chopped
¼ cup loosely packed mint leaves
¼ cup loosely packed cilantro leaves
1 ripe avocado, roughly chopped
¼ cup white onion, chopped
¼ teaspoon ground cumin
¼ teaspoon curry powder
2 tablespoons extra-virgin olive oil
¼ cup vegan mayonnaise or sour cream
2 teaspoons Dijon mustard
Juice of 2 limes plus more as needed
1½ teaspoons sea salt plus more as needed
1½ teaspoons black pepper
½ teaspoon agave syrup or granulated sugar
1 cup water

For the pumpkin seeds:

½ pound shelled, raw pumpkin seeds
2 teaspoons smoked paprika
1 teaspoon ground cumin
1 teaspoon sea salt
2 teaspoons olive oil

For serving:

Additional extra-virgin olive oil, as needed

To prepare the soup: Puree all ingredients in a food processor to a smooth, creamy consistency. Chill for 1 hour. Taste and adjust lime or salt as needed.

To prepare the pumpkin seeds: Preheat oven to 400°F. Toss pumpkin seeds with spices and oil and bake until seeds brown and become fragrant, 7 to 10 minutes. Set aside.

To serve: Pour soup into four bowls and garnish with pumpkin seeds and olive oil.

Oyster House

RITTENHOUSE SQUARE
1516 SANSOM STREET
(215) 567-7683
WWW.OYSTERHOUSEPHILLY.COM

The Oyster House feels of-the-moment—light and airy, lined with bright subway tiles—until you get a tour of the restaurant from owner Sam Mink. The milk-glass cocktail rail at the front of the restaurant was salvaged from Kelly's, a classic Philadelphia fish house that Mink's grandfather Samuel bought in 1947. The oyster plates hanging on the wall are part of the Mink family's two-hundred-plus plate collection, gathered through a half century of shucking. Server Lorraine Steele has been with the family for more than three decades, and that quirky Philadelphia favorite fried oyster and chicken salad has been on the menu just as long.

Mink's father, David, opened the original Sansom Street Oyster House in this spot in 1976 and ran it until his retirement in 2000. The business was sold and then shuttered. In 2009, Sam reopened the restaurant, in the same Sansom Street location, minus the Sansom Street name, reigniting the city's dying fish house tradition.

"There were no traditional fish houses left in Philadelphia," says the third-generation restaurateur. "I want to re-create the Oyster House for Philadelphia, with hints of the past while moving toward the future." So there's the snapper soup, a fish house standard too often known elsewhere for its thick cornstarch texture. At the Oyster House, the soup starts with whole snapping turtles, served with top-notch sherry from the bar.

"Old school, new school—we use those terms a lot," Mink says. "Oyster House bridges the gap."

Oyster Stew

"The traditional oyster stew is just oysters and cream, but we wanted something a little fresh and exciting for the new Oyster House," says Oyster House owner Sam Mink. "Anise flavors and oysters pair very well together so we add fennel to the stew and garnish it with tarragon. 'Shrubbery,' that's what some of the old-timers call the new stuff we've put in there. They request it 'without shrubbery,' just classic oysters and cream, which we are happy to do, too."

SERVES 4

1 tablespoon unsalted butter
2 cups sliced leeks
2 cups sliced fennel
6 cups heavy cream
1 tablespoon Worcestershire sauce
2 dashes Tabasco or other hot sauce
Kosher salt and black pepper, as needed
24 oysters, shucked
1 lemon, zested
2 tablespoons roughly chopped tarragon

In a large saucepan over medium heat, melt butter. Cook leeks and fennel until tender but not browned. Add heavy cream and cook over medium heat until the mixture has reduced enough to coat the back of a spoon, about 20 minutes. Add Worcestershire sauce and hot sauce. Season with salt and pepper.

Reduce heat to bring cream mixture to a simmer. Add oysters and their liquid. Poach gently until oysters plump in the middle and shrivel around the edges, 1 to 2 minutes. Add lemon zest and tarragon. Divide between four bowls and serve immediately.

BLANC & BLUE MARTINI
{OYSTER HOUSE}

"Super simple and light," says bartender Katie Loeb. "It's the perfect summer martini. I choose the Bluecoat gin because it's local, it's delicious, and most importantly its citrus-forward elements match so well with seafood."

SERVES 1

3 ounces Bluecoat gin
1 ounce Dolin Blanc vermouth
1 drop orange bitters
Ice
Lemon twist

Stir gin, vermouth, and bitters over ice until well chilled. Strain into a chilled cocktail glass. Twist lemon peel over drink to release citrus oils and drop peel into drink.

New England Clam Chowder

"Gulf Coast and West Coast oysters are fine, but we are an East Coast oyster bar," says Oyster House owner Sam Mink. "Our New England clam chowder is a staple dish for our East Coast–centric seafood menu. It's the perfect combination of briny clams, sweet cream, and creamy potatoes."

(Note: Chowder is best when made a day in advance.)

SERVES 4

12 cherrystone clams
4 cups clam juice
1 cup diced bacon
2 cups diced Spanish onion
2 cups diced celery
2 tablespoons unsalted butter
6 tablespoons all-purpose flour
2 sprigs thyme
1 bay leaf
2 cups diced russet potatoes
2 cups heavy cream
Kosher salt and black pepper, as needed

In a medium saucepan with a tight fitting lid, combine clams and clam juice. Cover and bring to a boil over high heat. Reduce heat to low and simmer until clams open, 10 to 15 minutes. Strain, reserving clams and clam stock. When cool, remove clams from shells and finely chop clams. Set aside.

In a separate medium saucepan over medium heat, cook bacon until fat renders and bacon crisps. Add onion and celery and sweat until softened but not browned, about 5 minutes.

Add butter. When butter melts, add flour and cook for 1 minute. Add thyme and bay leaf. Slowly add reserved clam stock, stirring, to avoid clumps. Lower heat and bring to a simmer, skimming any impurities that rise to the surface with a ladle.

Add potatoes and heavy cream and continue to simmer until potatoes are tender, 10 to 15 minutes. Remove herbs and season with salt and pepper. Add chopped clams.

ROUGE

RITTENHOUSE SQUARE
205 SOUTH 18TH STREET
(215) 732-6622
WWW.ROUGE98.COM

Oh, Rouge. There are so many stories to be told about Rouge (. . . engagements, weddings, affairs, divorces, celebrities canoodling in the corner . . .), each more outrageous than the next (. . . and then founder Neil Stein was imprisoned for tax evasion . . .). So much so that the only thing that can surprise people is that all of this—plus a ¾-pound burger that *GQ* ranked as one of "The 20 Hamburgers You Must Eat Before You Die"—happened in a dining room that's just eight hundred square feet.

Since its opening in 1998, Rouge has loomed far bigger in the psyche—and on the sidewalks—of Rittenhouse Square, spilling out onto 18th Street with coveted bistro tables that doubled the restaurant's seating capacity and launched the city's outdoor dining scene. The French-influenced restaurant transformed a former state liquor store into a never-ending cocktail party, hosted by the restaurant's regulars. To be a regular takes commitment—the most recognized faces have been frequenting the restaurant nearly daily for more than a dozen years—but the reward is a sidewalk seat facing the square on the first sunny spring day.

"Rouge has become a piece of the fabric of Philadelphia," says Rob Wasserman, who now owns the restaurant with his wife, Maggie (who also happens to be Neil Stein's daughter). "It's timeless."

BIBB & ENDIVE SALAD

"I created this dish in 1999, when a lot of people were doing a Bibb and endive salad. I wanted to do it a little differently, with spicy cashews," says Rouge chef Michael Yeamans. "The dish has stood the test of time. It is still one of our top sellers."

SERVES 4

For the spiced cashews (makes 3¼ cups):

3¼ cups unsalted cashews
1 tablespoon ground cumin
1 tablespoon paprika
½ tablespoon ground cayenne pepper
½ tablespoon chile powder
½ tablespoon kosher salt
½ tablespoon black pepper
½ cup granulated sugar
¼ cup hot water

For the red wine vinaigrette (makes 4¼ cups):

1 cup red wine vinegar
¼ cup Dijon mustard
2 tablespoons honey
Kosher salt and black pepper, as needed
2 cups vegetable oil
1 cup extra-virgin olive oil

For the salad:

2 endives
2 heads Bibb lettuce, separated into leaves
1 cup grape tomatoes, cut in half
½ cup julienned red onion
1 cup sliced apple
2 tablespoons minced shallot
2 tablespoons chopped flat-leaf parsley
2 tablespoons chopped chives
½ cup prepared red wine vinaigrette

For serving:

1 cup crumbled Roquefort cheese

To prepare the spiced cashews: Preheat oven to 300°F. In a large bowl, mix cashews with spices. In a separate bowl, combine sugar and water, mixing until sugar is dissolved. Add sugar water to cashews, stirring until fully combined. Spread cashews on a baking sheet and cook until nuts appear dry, about 15 minutes. Let cool.

To prepare the red wine vinaigrette: Whisk together red wine vinegar, mustard, and honey in a bowl. Season with salt and pepper. In a separate bowl, whisk together vegetable and olive oils. Slowly drizzle oil into vinegar mixture, whisking until emulsified.

To prepare the salad: Cut endives into quarters, lengthwise. Remove core and slice thinly lengthwise. Toss endive, lettuce, tomatoes, red onion, apple, shallots, parsley, and chives with red wine vinaigrette.

To serve: Divide salad between four plates. Garnish with cheese and 1 cup prepared spiced cashews.

MidAtlantic Restaurant & Tap Room

University City

Philadelphia first met Daniel Stern when the Cherry Hill native was named executive chef at Le Bec-Fin in 2002. He spent twenty months in Chef Georges Perrier's famed kitchen, helping the restaurant regain the fifth Mobil star it had lost a year earlier.

But Philadelphia didn't really get to know Stern until the chef set out on his own, first with Gayle and Rae (both shuttered) and later with chic R2L atop Liberty Place and Pennsylvania Dutch–inspired MidAtlantic in West Philly.

"I'm not much of a traditionalist," says Stern, a surprising statement to anyone who knows Le Bec-Fin's classic French style and an obvious one to anyone who has tasted Stern's smoked rabbit nachos, deconstructed veal stew, or endive parfait. "But I believe in going back to the roots of cuisine. That's the starting point."

At MidAtlantic, that process has produced crab scrapple with pepper jelly, fried clams with salsify, and Stern's ideal Philadelphia soft pretzel, served with house-made mustards.

"I'm not a traditionalist," Stern repeats. "I didn't set out saying this is a traditional Pennsylvania Dutch restaurant, but we have a strong regional cuisine with really strong flavors with a lot of historical foundation. From there, hopefully, we can start to make new traditions."

MIDATLANTIC RESTAURANT & TAP ROOM [2009–2012]

Unfortunately MidAtlantic closed its doors in 2012.

WHY WE'LL MISS IT: "MidAtlantic was a pioneering restaurant – not just in location, but in celebrating our region's food and flavors," says chef-owner Daniel Stern."

WHY IT CLOSED: No one is saying. Perhaps there is such a thing as too much scrapple?

WHAT COMES NEXT: Stern is in his kitchen at R2L, high atop Liberty Place.

Roasted Beet Jar

"Somewhere along the line, beets and goat cheese became something that people wanted to see on every restaurant menu," says MidAtlantic Restaurant & Tap Room chef-owner Daniel Stern. "We, of course, wanted to reinvent that, using the traditional ingredients in a new way. And the jar that we serve it in is a nod to the pickled vegetables that are a staple of the region."

SERVES 4

For the cider-walnut vinaigrette
(makes about 3 cups):

4 Bosc pears, peeled and cored
½ cup apple cider vinegar
¼ teaspoon Tabasco or other hot sauce
1 tablespoon Dijon mustard
1 teaspoon kosher salt
1½ cup grape seed oil
¼ cup walnut oil
¼ cup water

For the beets:

2 large red beets
4 tablespoons kosher salt, divided
1 cup red wine
2 bay leaves, divided
4 sprigs thyme, divided
20 black peppercorns, divided
6 cups water, divided
2 large yellow beets
1 cup white wine
1 teaspoon finely chopped flat-leaf parsley
1 teaspoon finely chopped chives
2 teaspoons sherry vinegar
1 tablespoon extra-virgin olive oil

For the croutons:

2 tablespoons unsalted butter, melted
1 cup 1-inch cubes angel food cake
Kosher salt and black pepper, as needed

For the greens:

2 cup mixed greens
¼ cup prepared cider-walnut vinaigrette
2 tablespoons chopped toasted walnuts

For serving:

1 cup 1-inch cubes goat cheese (MidAtlantic uses
    Shellbark Hollow Farm)

To prepare the cider-walnut vinaigrette: In a food processor, puree pears, vinegar, hot sauce, mustard, and salt. In a bowl, combine grape seed and walnut oils. Slowly drizzle oil into pear mixture while processing. Add water in a constant stream while processing.

To prepare the beets: In a large saucepan over low heat, combine red beets, 2 tablespoons kosher salt, 1 cup red wine, 1 bay leaf, 2 sprigs thyme, 10 black peppercorns, and 3 cups water. In a separate large saucepan, combine 2 large yellow beets, remaining 2 tablespoons kosher salt, 1 cup white wine, remaining 1 bay leaf, remaining 2 thyme sprigs, remaining 10 peppercorns, and remaining 3 cups water.

Bring both mixtures to a simmer and cook red and yellow beets until tender, about 3 hours. Remove beets and allow to cool. Remove skins by rubbing beets with a paper towel. Dice red and yellow beets into 1-inch cubes.

In a bowl, combine beets, parsley, chives, sherry vinegar, and olive oil.

To prepare the croutons: Preheat oven to 350°F. Brush butter on all sides of angel food cake cubes and season with salt and pepper. Bake until angel food croutons are golden brown.

To prepare the greens: In a bowl, combine mixed greens, cider-walnut vinaigrette, and walnuts.

To serve: Place greens in the bottom of four jars or on four plates, and top with beets. Crumble goat cheese over beets and garnish with croutons.

THE INGREDIENTS: SHELLBARK HOLLOW FARM

It has become fashionable in recent years to detail the origin of each ingredient on a menu, to carefully catalog the names of once-obscure farms. For the average diner, the names mean little—until they taste the goat cheeses made by Shellbark Hollow Farm in West Chester.

You'll see it on the menu at Talula's Garden (page 89), Meritage (page 18), and MidAtlantic Restaurant & Tap Room, where chef-owner Daniel Stern uses the cubes of the rich, tangy cheese in his Roasted Beet Jar salad (page 63). And you'll see the cheesemonger's favorite at home-cook haunts like Di Bruno Bros., Fair Food Farmstand, and area farmers' markets.

Farmer Pete Demsher's secret isn't much of a secret: sixteen years of experience raising a herd of lovable Nubian goats. (Farm favorites earn the "goat of the month" nod on the farm's blog.) The long-eared goats produce milk that is high in butterfat, perfect for making the farm's signature chèvre spreads—the sharp garlic chive chèvre is quick to sell out at farmers' markets—and its award-winning dry sharp chèvre. The farm is also making a name for itself with raw milk, kefir, and yogurt.
www.shellbarkhollow.com

Parc

Rittenhouse Square
227 South 18th Street
(215) 545-2262
www.parc-restaurant.com

Parc, Stephen Starr's sprawling, spectacular French brasserie on Rittenhouse Square, was almost a deli.

"That's what the owners of the building originally wanted," says Starr, a restaurateur renowned for his endless supply of restaurant concepts. He pauses to consider: "This isn't that much different from a deli, really."

Age-tarnished mirrors, salvaged brass fixtures, French-language newspapers, and the city's best baguette aside, Starr has a point: The bistro is France's answer to the deli, serving up a classic menu, three meals a day, in a casual, convivial environment. Plus—this is key—a bar, the same gleaming zinc beacon you'd find in a Paris classic.

And then there's the inimitable location, stretching down 18th Street along the park—those bistro chairs, all turned to face Rittenhouse Square, a warming sight even on blustery winter days—and turning on to quieter Locust Street, where *en plein air* diners might hear the city's next protégé practicing at the Curtis Institute of Music.

At 7:30 a.m., the restaurant is a quiet refuge for an omelet and a café au lait. At noon, it is business meetings over *moules frites*. At 3 p.m., people watching and onion soup gratinée. At 5 p.m., happy-hour cocktails and oysters. At 8 p.m., lingering over steak frites and roast chicken, crème brûlée and tarte tatin, and a carafe of wine. Weekend brunch—sleep in, the restaurant doesn't even open its doors until 10—is croissants, Champagne, and towers of fruits de mer.

"Breakfast, lunch, or dinner. This is where you bring your friends and celebrate your life," says Starr.

SALADE LYONNAISE

"This is a very, very classic dish in French cooking, and it's my favorite salad on the menu," says Parc chef Michael Abt. "It all mixes very well. Egg yolks and bacon help to cut the acid of the dressing and the bitterness of the greens."

SERVES 4

3 ½-inch-thick slices brioche, crust removed,
   cut in 1-inch cubes
½ cup plus 2 tablespoons olive oil, divided
Kosher salt and black pepper, as needed
½ cup sherry vinegar
1½ teaspoons Dijon mustard
½ cup vegetable oil
1 tablespoon white vinegar
4 large eggs
2 tablespoons unsalted butter
½ pound bacon, cut in ½-inch cubes
2 russet potatoes, cut in ½-inch cubes
8 cups torn frisée, dark green leaves discarded
⅓ cup flat-leaf parsley leaves
⅓ cup tarragon leaves
⅓ cup chervil leaves
1 shallot, finely chopped

Preheat oven to 350°F. To make croutons, toss bread cubes with 2 tablespoons olive oil and sprinkle with salt and pepper. Spread in a single layer on a baking sheet and bake, turning once, until golden brown, about 10 minutes.

To make the vinaigrette, combine sherry vinegar and mustard. In a separate bowl, combine remaining ½ cup olive oil and vegetable oil. Slowly pour oil mixture into vinegar mixture, whisking vigorously until emulsified.

To poach eggs, bring a large saucepan filled with water to a simmer. Add white vinegar. Gently slide the eggs, one at a time, into the simmering water. (See "Step by Step," page 69.) Cook until whites are just set, about 4 minutes. Lift poached eggs out of water with a slotted spoon and place in a bowl of warm water until serving.

In a sauté pan over medium heat, melt butter until sizzling. Add bacon and cook slowly until crisp on all sides, about 10 minutes. Remove bacon. Add potatoes to bacon fat in sauté pan and cook until golden brown. Remove potatoes, sprinkle with salt, and drain on paper towels.

In a large bowl, combine frisée, parsley, tarragon, chervil, and shallots. Add bacon, potatoes, and croutons and toss together. Drizzle salad with vinaigrette and toss. Divide salad between four plates. Place a poached egg at the center of each plate and serve.

STEP BY STEP: POACHING AN EGG

"Poaching an egg isn't hard, but it does take some practice," says Parc chef Michael Abt. "Poach one egg at a time until you get used to the process."

1. HEAT

In a saucepan, combine 8 cups of water and 1 tablespoon white vinegar. The vinegar will help keep the egg whites from spreading during cooking. Heat to 180°F, which is barely simmering.

2. CRACK

Crack eggs into individual bowls. This prevents egg shells from falling into the poaching water and allows you to add the eggs to the water more gently.

3. SWIRL

With a spoon, swirl heated water to form a whirlpool. The motion will keep the egg whites close to the egg yolk and prevent the egg from dropping to the bottom of the pan.

4. COOK

Carefully add egg to swirling water. Cook for 4 minutes. Remove from water with a slotted spoon and drain on a paper towel. Gently press egg with one finger to ensure that the whites are set and the yolk remains liquid.

5. SERVE

Serve immediately or allow to cool, returning poached eggs to barely simmering water until reheated before serving.

TRIA

TWO LOCATIONS: RITTENHOUSE SQUARE AND WASHINGTON SQUARE WEST
18TH AND SANSOM STREETS, (215) 972-8742
12TH AND SPRUCE STREETS, (215) 629-9200
WWW.TRIACAFE.COM

Even Tria owner Jon Myerow seems surprised by the success of this small wine, beer, and cheese bar. "It's amazing to me that some of our top-selling wines are varietals that people 'don't' drink, like Chenin Blanc and Zweigelt," he says. That was the goal from the start: to introduce Philadelphia, already starting to discover craft beers, to artisanal beers, wines, and cheeses, without any of the pretension that comes with the words "wine bar." (And without the signature cocktails that were a mainstay of the Rittenhouse Square scene; Myerow recalls that when the restaurant opened in 2004, the first customer tried to order a cosmo.)

One popular Chenin Blanc is described on the frequently changing menu in a mixture of traditional wine speak and honest enthusiasm: "Redolent of honeyed pear, fig, and citrus with a mineral rich finish from the man, Bruwer Raats." Cheeses are "ice cream for grown-ups" (a beer-washed cow's-milk cheese from Wisconsin), a "cream-infused pillow" (classic Brillat-Savarin from France), and "eminently lemony and fresh" (a Massachusetts goat's-milk cheese). Beer is categorized from "invigorating" to "extreme." No matter the adjectives, the offerings all have one thing in common. "Everything is made by real people," Myerow says.

The Tria vibe—99 percent enjoyment, 1 percent education—caught on quickly. A second Tria location followed, and the restaurant launched the Tria Fermentation School to offer wine, beer, and cheese classes. In 2010, Biba—now renamed Tria Wine Room—opened in West Philly, an impossibly smaller take on the Tria model.

"When we opened Tria, there was nothing else like it," says Myerow. "There's still not enough places like it."

GRILLED ASPARAGUS SALAD

"Our menu is hard to define. We call it 'wine bar cuisine' because it is a little Spanish, a little Italian, a little of all of the Mediterranean countries you think of as wine countries," says Tria owner Jon Myerow. "It's all of those things, and this salad is a great example because it has all of those Mediterranean flavors."

SERVES 4

2 tablespoons smooth Dijon mustard
¼ cup red wine vinegar
1½ cups canola oil
Kosher salt and black pepper, as needed
1 pint grape tomatoes, sliced into thirds
1 roasted red bell pepper, diced
2 tablespoons chopped red onion
12 stalks asparagus, trimmed, grilled, cooled, and cut into 1½-inch pieces

1 cup sliced Ruggiero or other Italian-marinated artichokes
2 cups Divina or other white beans
4 large slices rustic whole wheat bread
2 tablespoons extra-virgin olive oil, divided
3 tablespoons pine nuts, toasted
1 lemon

In a blender or food processor, combine mustard and vinegar. While processing, slowly add oil until emulsified. Season vinaigrette with salt and pepper. Combine vinaigrette with tomatoes, red bell pepper, and onion, mixing well to coat. Allow relish to sit at least 1 hour. (It can be made up to 2 days in advance.)

In a large bowl combine asparagus, artichokes, and white beans. Using a slotted spoon, scoop relish onto salad. Add vinaigrette to taste.

Brush bread with 1 tablespoon olive oil and grill or toast until edges are crisp. Cut each slice into thirds and arrange in the center of each plate. Spoon salad on top of bread. Garnish with remaining 1 tablespoon olive oil, pine nuts, and a squeeze of lemon juice.

KANELLA

WASHINGTON SQUARE WEST
1001 SPRUCE STREET
(215) 922-1773
WWW.KANELLARESTAURANT.COM

Kanella opened the doors to its simple, white washed dining room on April 27, 2008, Greek Easter Sunday—"for a little luck," chef-owner Konstantinos Pitsillides says, and the superstition has paid off for the popular BYOB.

This isn't a Greek restaurant as you might know it. The fiercely authentic chef shudders at the stereotype of Americanized Greek food and draws the distinction even more brightly: "A lot of people think that this is a Greek-Greek restaurant, but it is a Cypriot-Greek restaurant, which means more spice and Middle Eastern influences."

Pitsillides is Cypriot, born in the coastal city of Limassol. His wife is Philadelphian, which explains how the flavors and philosophy of Pitsillides's Mediterranean upbringing arrived at the corner of 10th and Spruce. "This is the simple food I grew up with," Pitsillides says.

The opinionated chef has a lot more to say. He'll rail against new trends that aren't new at all or chefs who spend their time whining instead of cooking, often in missives posted in his kitchen window. But the food at Kanella—warm hummus topped with ground lamb, whole fish with seasonal greens, spice-braised goat—is as much of a statement as Pitsillides's handwritten philosophy on simplicity: "Simplicity is to eschew garish taste and over-elaboration."

WATERMELON SALAD WITH FETA & ALMONDS

"We often create dishes by accident—and by tomorrow I won't remember what I did tonight, so we're changing things everyday," says Kanella chef-owner Konstantinos Pitsillides. "I had a watermelon and in my country we often pair it with *halloumi*. Here I used feta. I like the sweetness of the watermelon, the salty sourness of the anchovies, and the freshness of the greens with the creaminess of the feta."

SERVES 4

1 cup water
½ cup granulated sugar
¼ cup rose water (available at Middle Eastern markets)
¼ cup extra-virgin olive oil
½ large, heavy watermelon, flesh cut in medium cubes
1 yellow tomato, chopped

20 white anchovies (available at Italian markets)
½ cup slivered almonds, toasted
1/3 pound Greek feta
½ cup mint leaves
1 cup scallions, finely chopped
Kosher salt, as needed
1 teaspoon black pepper

In a saucepan over medium-high heat, combine water, sugar, and rose water. Cook until sugar dissolves and mixture begins to thickens, about 15 minutes. Chill. Whisk in olive oil to emulsify.

Toss watermelon and tomato with rose water mixture. Arrange watermelon and tomato on a platter and top with anchovies, almonds, crumbled feta, mint, and scallions. Season with salt and pepper.

Pastas

Philadelphia is a pasta town. Red gravy is a religion in some segments of South Philly. It's hard to compete with *nonna*, but the city's best (and, perhaps, bravest) chefs have made their mark with pastas that go beyond the Sunday dinner table.

A new pasta culture is taking shape—and it is taking every shape, from common spaghetti, pappardelle, and ravioli to less-familiar *tesaroli* (a crepe-style noodle) and *tortelli* (a half-moon take on ravioli). In their pasta dishes, Philadelphia chefs are exploring all of Italy, drawing inspiration from Rome, Lombardy, and Tuscany, but their culinary travels don't end there.

Talula's Garden adopts potato gnocchi to celebrate the mushroom harvest of nearby Kennett Square (page 89), and Buddakan goes around the world to transform the ravioli with edamame (page 84). Han Dynasty reminds us that Italy doesn't have a hold on the world's great noodles with the Szechuan classic Dan Dan Noodles (page 95), and Paradiso takes dinner back to South Philly with the linguine and clams chef Lynn Rinaldi recalls from her East Passyunk childhood (page 86).

VETRI

WASHINGTON SQUARE WEST
1312 SPRUCE STREET
(215) 732-3478
WWW.VETRIRISTORANTE.COM

Marc Vetri, modestly describes his goals when he opened Vetri in 1998: "I just wanted to open a nice, little, inviting restaurant like the ones I had been seeing all over Italy." The location, a Washington Square West row home, gave the restaurant that intimate feel—"I wanted it to feel like you were eating in my living room"—and a culinary destiny to fulfill. Vetri's "living room" was the original home of the city's most famous restaurant, Le Bec-Fin.

Vetri was up to the challenge. The restaurant's miniature kitchen has produced memorable dishes—his spinach gnocchi in brown butter, *foie gras* pastrami, and asparagus flan are classics—and launched a new generation of Philadelphia chefs, from Vetri partners Jeff Michaud (Osteria, page 108) and Brad Spence (Amis, page 28) to Michael Solomonov of Zahav (page 115) and Dionicio Jimenez of El Rey (page 110). A Saturday night reservation for the chef's elaborate tasting menu was the hardest reservation in town—until Vetri transitioned to a tasting-menu-only concept every night.

"Vetri has never stopped evolving," says Vetri. "I've never had to force anything. I've just basically allowed the diners of Philadelphia to make the decisions."

Their decisions have placed that nice, little restaurant at the center of the Philadelphia food world, earning national praise for its James Beard award–winning chef and attention for the city's dining scene. Vetri is "possibly the best Italian restaurant on the East Coast," raves chef Mario Batali, who has a couple of his own Italian spots competing for that title.

SPAGHETTI WITH GREEN TOMATOES & RAZOR CLAMS

"We did this for one of our tasting menus," says Vetri chef-owner Marc Vetri. "We were just kind of messing around. Razor clams have this awesome sweet flavor, and we wanted to think of something that was going to balance it out. Fleshy green tomatoes have a little extra acid and a little bit of a sour flavor, and it worked perfectly. The green tomatoes cook down to make a natural mignonette for the clams."

SERVES 4

4 green tomatoes
¼ cup extra-virgin olive oil
1 shallot, diced
½ clove garlic
Kosher salt, as needed
½ pound spaghetti
5 razor clams
Additional extra-virgin olive oil, as needed

To peel tomatoes cut a shallow *x* on the bottom of the tomatoes. Dip tomatoes in boiling water for 10 seconds and then shock them in an ice water bath. Remove and peel. Dice tomatoes.

In a large saucepan over medium heat, heat olive oil. Add shallot and garlic and cook until softened but not browned. Remove garlic and add tomatoes. Cook tomatoes until soft, stirring constantly to prevent browning, about 10 minutes. Reduce heat to low and keep sauce warm.

Bring a large saucepan of heavily salted water to a boil over high heat. Add spaghetti and cook for 2 minutes less than package instructions.

As pasta cooks, open razor clams by sliding a butter knife along open side of shell. Use knife to remove clam. Rinse clams. Coat clams with olive oil and season with salt. Slice clams into pieces as big as coffee beans.

When pasta is done, drain, reserving 1 cup pasta water. Add pasta and reserved pasta water to sauce. Cook over high heat for 2 minutes. Toss with clams and season with salt.

Morimoto

WASHINGTON SQUARE WEST
723 CHESTNUT STREET
(215) 413-9070
WWW.MORIMOTORESTAURANT.COM

When Morimoto opened in 2001, this Stephen Starr restaurant wowed with its Tokyo-sleek decor, its toro tartare, flavored with house-made soy sauce and freshly grated wasabi, and its omakase menu. The multicourse meal of small dishes—with most of the fish shipped overnight from Tsukiji, Tokyo's famous fish market and prepared by chef Masaharu Morimoto himself—was one of Philadelphia's must-have dining experiences.

Ponytailed and broad-shouldered, chef Morimoto was a striking presence behind the restaurant's sushi bar, wielding his knives to create sushi in the traditional style he learned in his native Japan, with a little *Iron Chef* flair. "You need a sharp knife and a sharp arm," the

former baseball player often says. On both the original Japanese cult hit and the later Food Network remake, Morimoto also showed a sharp sense of flavor and a willingness to experiment with it. In Kitchen Stadium, he was known for adding Chinese, French, Italian, and other global flavors to create *Iron Chef*-winning dishes. A Morimoto favorite: soba noodle carbonara. "I don't believe in rules," Morimoto says.

More than ten years later, chef Morimoto has opened five more restaurants around the world—including one in New York with Starr—and is better known for his big gestures than his small ones. His visits to Philadelphia might involve carving a two hundred-pound tuna or hosting a big-ticket private charity dinner. But the Iron Chef's influence is strong, and the restaurant remains the city's top sushi spot.

SOBA CARBONARA

"I always say, 'My father is Japanese, but my mother is Italian,'" says Morimoto chef Masaharu Morimoto. "Of course, it's a joke, but I have a lot of recipes in which Italian essence is used, so I have to explain why I use Italian ingredients or techniques to the curious audience. I don't see any boundaries in cooking, so I just thought carbonara sauce should go with soba noodles, too."

SERVES 4

½ pound dry soba noodles
1 tablespoon olive oil
3 slices bacon, chopped
½ cup boiled edamame, shelled
24 bay scallops
2 tablespoons white wine
¼ cup water
1 tablespoon soy sauce
1¼ cups heavy cream
3 large egg yolks, beaten
Dash of truffle oil
Kosher salt and white pepper, as needed
Parmesan cheese, as needed

Special equipment: Thermometer

In a large saucepan of boiling salted water, cook soba noodles for 1 minute less than the package directions. Drain well. Toss with olive oil and set aside.

In a large sauté pan over medium heat, cook bacon until fat renders. Remove bacon and drain on paper towels. In the same sauté pan over medium heat, cook edamame and scallops until heated, 2 to 3 minutes. Add bacon. Turn off heat.

In a saucepan over medium heat, cook white wine to evaporate alcohol. Add water, soy sauce, and cream, and heat to 155°F. Add egg yolks and truffle oil. Season with salt and white pepper. Turn the heat to low and whisk until smooth, being careful not to let the egg yolks cook through. Add reserved bacon, edamame, and scallops and stir. Add soba and stir quickly.

Divide between four pasta bowls and sprinkle with cheese.

JAMES

ITALIAN MARKET

One dish tells the whole story of James.

The restaurant's signature Risotto alla Kristina is not the rich, creamy risotto we've become accustomed to. Instead it is light and brothy, a lesser-known Venetian style that is subtle and surprising. That's James chef-owner Jim Burke's style (pictured at right)—subtle and surprising—as evidenced by this elegant, modern almost-Italian restaurant amid the hubbub of the traditional Italian Market.

The Risotto Alla Kristina is studded with briny oysters and sparked with Prosecco. That's Burke's wife, Kristina's style. She is the inspiration for the dish that bears her name and the restaurant's bubbly hostess.

And the Risotto alla Kristina is laden with accolades—it was named one of *Food & Wine*'s Best Restaurant Dishes of 2007—as has been the restaurant's style since its opening that same year.

The intimate, well-designed spot—neither the storefront BYOB nor the big Starr production that dominated the restaurant scene at the time—earned those raves with its risotto and dishes like roasted Four Story Hill Farm poularde and duck ragu topped with dark chocolate grated tableside, and even its desserts, with classic, but not common, combinations like chocolate, olive oil, and sea salt.

JAMES [2007–2011]

Unfortunately James closed its doors in 2011.

WHY WE'LL MISS IT: "James was a personal expression of what we love," says James chef-owner Jim Burke. "We poured all of ourselves into it."

WHY IT CLOSED: "We were never really in love with the location," says Burke. "As the economy got worse, the location became more and more of an issue."

WHAT COMES NEXT: Burke headed to New York to open a new Stephen Starr restaurant in the New York Historical Society. The duck ragu and Risotto alla Kristina went with him.

Pappardelle with Duck Ragu, Chocolate & Orange

"I remembered a dish like this from the restaurant I worked at in Italy," says James chef-owner Jim Burke. "It's a perfect reflection of my philosophy of cooking: It has complex, deep flavors, but it is really a simple combination—the chocolate pairs so well with duck, and the orange has a way of lifting the dish—and the cooking technique highlights the ingredients."

SERVES 4

1 navel orange
4 duck legs, skin removed
Kosher salt and black pepper, as needed
1 tablespoon all-purpose flour
1 tablespoon olive oil
5 tablespoons unsalted butter, divided
2 tablespoons finely diced onion
1 tablespoon finely diced carrot
1 tablespoon finely diced celery
2 cups dry red wine
1 cup port
2 cups chicken stock
¼ cup chopped 70 percent chocolate
1 pound fresh pappardelle (see "Step by Step," page 83)
1 cup grated Parmesan cheese

Remove half the zest from the orange with a peeler, removing any pith. Remove the other half of the zest with a zester. Spread grated zest on a paper towel in a warm place to dry. Reserve orange flesh.

Season duck generously with salt and pepper. Dust lightly with flour, shaking off any excess flour. Choose a heavy-bottomed saucepan with a lid that will snugly fit the duck in one layer. Over medium heat, heat 1 tablespoon olive oil. When the olive oil is hot but not yet smoking, add duck. Brown deeply on all sides. When duck is fully browned, remove from pan and discard fat.

Add 1 tablespoon butter to pan. Add onion, carrot, celery, and peeled orange zest. Season with salt. Deeply brown vegetables over medium heat. Return duck to pan. Add juice from one-half orange. With a wooden spoon scrape caramelized pieces from the pan, cooking until juice is gone.

Add red wine and port. Increase heat to bring mixture to a boil, and then reduce heat so mixture simmers steadily. Simmer, partially covered, until mixture is reduced by one-third. Add chicken stock and reduce heat to bring to a low simmer. Simmer, partially covered, until meat begins to separate from the bone. Remove from heat and cool to room temperature. Remove duck and shred meat, discarding bones.

Return duck to pan. Warm ragu over low heat. Add chocolate, slowly, stirring to blend, tasting frequently. Remove peeled orange zest from ragu. Keep ragu warm.

Fill a large saucepan with water and salt heavily. Bring to a boil over high heat. Add pappardelle, stirring immediately to prevent sticking. Cook for 1 minute and taste. Remove when cooked through, reserving 1 cup pasta water. Add pappardelle to ragu with remaining 4 tablespoons butter and cheese. Cook for 30 seconds, stirring gently. Add reserved pasta water as needed to loosen ragu. Season with salt. Divide between four bowls and garnish with dried grated orange zest.

STEP BY STEP: MAKING PASTA

"Mixing pasta by hand is a lot of fun and very satisfying, but you can also do it in an electric
mixer," says James chef-owner Jim Burke. "You will need a pasta machine, though. You have
to be an Italian grandmother to do it with a rolling pin."

1. FIND

Start with 1 pound 00 flour, a soft wheat flour indigenous to northern Italy, available at Italian
markets or gourmet stores. All-purpose flour will work, too, but 00 is traditional for pasta made
with eggs.

2. COMBINE

Mound flour on a wooden surface (which maintains a good temperature for pasta making) and
form a deep well in the center. Crack 2 whole large eggs and 10 large egg yolks into a bowl.
Pour eggs into well. Using two fingers, stir circles in the eggs, slowly widening the circles to
incorporate flour, mimicking the motions of the electric mixer. The dough will slowly thicken
and form a ball.

3. KNEAD

Knead the dough with the heel of the dominant hand. Press the heel into the dough, stretching
the dough, then fold the dough on itself, give it a quarter turn, and repeat. Always knead, fold,
and turn in the same direction to promote the production of long gluten strands and tender
pasta. Continue kneading until a dry but smooth dough forms. If the dough remains wet, knead
in a little flour; if dry enough to crack, knead in a few drops of water.

4. OR, USE A MIXER

Instead, add flour to the bowl of an electric mixer fitted with a dough hook. Crack 2 whole
eggs and 10 egg yolks into a separate bowl. Start the mixer at medium and add eggs while
mixing. Continue to mix until dough is smooth and uniform and forms a football-like shape.

5. REST

Wrap the pasta dough in plastic wrap and rest at room temperature for 30 minutes or refrigerate for later use.

6. ROLL

Use a pasta machine to create the desired pasta shape. One pound flour will yield 4 to 6 portions. For pappardelle, roll the dough thinly and cut into long ¾-inch-thick ribbons.

Buddakan

Old City
325 Chestnut Street
(215) 574-9440
www.buddakan.com

Buddakan just might deserve credit for starting it all.

It wasn't Stephen Starr's first restaurant nor was it his first success—both of those distinctions go to the Continental, his Rat Pack martini lounge that relaunched Old City in 1995—but Buddakan's opening in 1998 marked a change in how Philadelphia thought about dining. As quickly as lines formed under the watchful gaze of an eleven-foot gold Buddha, restaurants were exciting and sexy again. No longer were Philadelphians content with just a meal. Buddakan taught diners and the countless future restaurateurs who worked there that dinner was an experience, be it a Hollywood-style Stephen Starr production or an indie BYOB.

It changed how Starr thought about dining, too: "I wasn't really a restaurateur yet, then," says the former concert promoter. "I didn't take it seriously that this was the beginning of a restaurant career for me." Since Buddakan opened its doors, Starr has opened more than twenty other restaurants in Philadelphia—from funky Mexican El Rey (page 110) to classic English pub The Dandelion (page 137) to local-focused Talula's Garden (page 89)—and expanded to other East Coast cities, including opening reincarnations of scene-changing Buddakan in Atlantic City's The Pier Shops at Caesars and New York's Meatpacking District.

Edamame Ravioli

"I consider the edamame ravioli to be the signature dish at Buddakan," says Buddakan owner Stephen Starr. "It is unique to us and what we do. When we opened Buddakan New York, we created lighter Edamame Dumplings for that restaurant."

SERVES 4

For the ravioli:

5 tablespoons unsalted butter, divided
6 shallots, thinly sliced
1²/₃ cups chicken stock
Kosher salt and white pepper, as needed
1 pound shelled edamame beans
¼ cup heavy cream
2 tablespoons white truffle oil
32 round wonton wrappers (available at Asian markets)

For the Sauternes-shallot broth:

1½ teaspoons butter
½ cup thinly sliced shallots
½ cup Sauternes wine
1²/₃ cups edamame-chicken broth (reserved from preparing ravioli)
2 sprigs thyme
Kosher salt and white pepper, as needed

To prepare the ravioli: In a medium saucepan over medium high heat, melt 3 tablespoons butter and cook shallots until caramelized. Add chicken stock and season with salt and white pepper. Add edamame beans to broth. Increase heat and bring mixture to a boil. Reduce heat and simmer until beans are tender, 10 to 15 minutes.

In a small saucepan over medium heat, combine cream and remaining 2 tablespoons butter. Drain beans, reserving beans and broth. (Broth will be used to make Sauternes-shallot broth.) In a food processor, puree beans, working in batches if necessary. Add cream mixture and continue to puree. Transfer beans to a bowl and add truffle oil, mixing well.

Lay out 16 wonton wrappers. Divide filling between wrappers, placing filling in the center of wonton wrapper. Brush edge of each wonton with water and place another wonton wrapper on top, pressing edges together to seal ravioli.

Fill a large saucepan with water. Bring to a boil over high heat. Cook ravioli for 2½ minutes.

To prepare the Sauternes-shallot broth: In a medium saucepan over medium-high heat, melt butter. Cook shallots in butter until caramelized. Add wine and reduce mixture by one-third. Add broth and thyme and simmer for 30 minutes. Remove thyme and season with salt and pepper. Set aside.

To serve: Divide ravioli between four plates and top with Sauternes-shallot broth.

Paradiso

South Philly
1627 East Passyunk Avenue
(215) 271-2066
www.paradisophilly.com

Lynn Rinaldi remembers East Passyunk Avenue as it used to be. She grew up just two blocks away, on 12th Street, in the '70s and '80s, when the avenue was bustling with mom-and-pop shops. So, when the longtime chef was ready to open her own restaurant, she looked to East Passyunk. "Everyone told me I was crazy," Rinaldi remembers. "East Passyunk was dead."

Rinaldi ignored everyone, opening 170-seat Paradiso in a vacant furniture store in 2004—and becoming one of the first sparks in an ongoing revitalization that has made East Passy a top dining destination. There are now ten restaurants on this block of East Passyunk alone, including Rinaldi's sushi destination Izumi, noted gelateria Capogiro (page 176), and South Philly standbys like Mr. Martino's Trattoria.

Opening a new Italian restaurant in a neighborhood known for its old Italian joints was "intimidating," Rinaldi, a former caterer, says, "but I didn't want to be one of those traditional South Philly restaurants." Paradiso distinguished itself not by updating Italian classics but by challenging the red gravy spots with handmade pastas, locally grown ingredients (figs and honey come from the garden and hives on the restaurant's roof), and old-school dishes like rabbit cacciatore and tripe.

"My dad said, 'Those are two things I love that you are probably never going to sell,'" Rinaldi says. Now, Paradiso is a mainstay of the newly bustling avenue, and the rabbit and tripe are the only dishes that remain unchanged from the opening day menu.

Linguine with Cockles

"My mother made macaroni and clams every Friday night," says Paradiso chef-owner Lynn Rinaldi. "She did it differently, of course. She went to Ippolito's, and they shucked the whole clams. I use the cockles, which open quickly and are sweeter, but the elements of this dish are still really simple. It's something you can make in 15 minutes and feed your whole family."

SERVES 4

4 tablespoons kosher salt
1 pound dry linguine fini
1 cup extra-virgin olive oil
6 ounces pancetta, diced small
4 cloves garlic, finely chopped

1 pound cockles, rinsed
½ cup dry white wine
1 tablespoon red pepper flakes
Additional kosher salt and black pepper, as needed
½ cup finely chopped flat-leaf parsley

Fill a large saucepan with water and 4 table-spoons salt and bring to a boil over high heat. Add linguine and cook according to package directions.

In a large sauté pan over medium heat, heat olive oil and pancetta. Cook until pancetta browns. Increase heat to high, and add garlic and cockles.

As cockles begin to open, add wine and red pepper flakes. Season with salt and pepper.

Drain linguine, reserving 1 cup cooking water. When cockles have opened, transfer linguine to sauté pan. Toss pasta to coat with sauce, adding reserved cooking water as needed. Top with parsley and serve.

Butternut Squash Tortelli

"This dish represents fall to me. You can use pumpkin, but I love butternut squash. It's savory, but a little sweet, too," says Paradiso chef-owner Lynn Rinaldi. "Sometimes I drain the roasted butternut squash in a colander overnight. The filling shouldn't be so loose that when you cut into it everything squirts out."

SERVES 4

2 cups 00 flour (available at gourmet stores)
Pinch of kosher salt
4 large eggs, lightly beaten, divided
3 tablespoons extra-virgin olive oil, divided
4 cups peeled, seeded, and chopped butternut
    squash
1 cup Parmesan cheese, divided
2 cups ricotta
1 cup bread crumbs
Kosher salt and black pepper, as needed
6 tablespoons unsalted butter
8 sage leaves

Special equipment: Pasta roller and 3-inch
    cookie cutter

Sift flour and salt into a mound on the counter. Make a well in center of flour and add 2 eggs and 1 tablespoon olive oil. Using your fingers, slowly incorporate flour until dough forms, adding additional flour if dough seems sticky. (See "Step by Step," page 83.) Shape dough into a ball and knead until smooth to the touch, about 15 minutes. Wrap dough in plastic wrap and rest in refrigerator for 30 minutes.

Preheat oven to 375°F. Toss butternut squash in remaining 2 tablespoons olive oil. Bake until softened, 45 minutes. In a food processor, puree butternut squash, working in batches as needed. In a bowl, combine pureed butternut squash, remaining 2 eggs, ¾ cup Parmesan cheese, ricotta, and bread crumbs to make filling. Season with salt and pepper.

Roll pasta dough into thin sheets with a pasta roller. On a floured surface, use a 3-inch cookie cutter to form pasta rounds. Spoon 1 tablespoon of filling into the center of each round. Fold in half and crimp edges of dough together to form tortelli.

Bring a saucepan of salted water to a boil. Cook tortelli for 5 minutes.

In a sauté pan over medium-high heat, melt butter. Add sage. Drain tortelli and add tortelli to skillet. Toss to coat with butter. Divide between plates and top with remaining ¼ cup Parmesan cheese.

Talula's Garden

Washington Square
210 West Washington Square
(215) 592-7787
www.talulasgarden.com

It started with Django, the petite South Street spot that became the benchmark for the Philadelphia BYOB—and the first to receive *Philadelphia Inquirer* food critic Craig LaBan's top four-bell rating. Next Aimee Olexy (pictured below) and her then-husband, Bryan Sikora, sold Django and moved their talents to Kennett Square, where they opened Talula's Table,

a cozy cafe and gourmet food shop by day and the nation's toughest reservation after dark. The single farmhouse table—seating twelve—is booked a year in advance. Finally, Olexy returned to Philadelphia to open Talula's Garden with restaurateur Stephen Starr.

Talula's Garden brings a little of Chester County to the city, its dining room extending into the garden courtyard overlooking Washington Square, and the garden extending back into the dining room with tomatoes and herbs flourishing under growing lights. It conjures the fondly remembered Django, with Olexy playing the gracious hostess and a smart, seasonal menu.

And, of course, there is the cheese. Olexy's cheese plate, which she annotated fervently for each table, was a must-order at Django. At Talula's Table, there are the cheese cases, filled with more than one hundred of Olexy's gooey, sharp, stinky favorites. And at Talula's Garden there is, as Olexy calls it, "my land of cheese," a salvaged granite counter with a dedicated cheesemonger that is the centerpiece of the restaurant.

Potato Gnocchi with Mushrooms & Egg

"This turns your idea of a gnocchi dish upside down," says Talula's Garden owner Aimee Olexy. "It is very light for a gnocchi dish, and you can really taste the potatoes. All the flavors go really well together—and egg is such a great, natural way to enrich the dish—but you can still taste the individual ingredients."

SERVES 6

For the potato gnocchi:

4 Yukon Gold potatoes
2 large egg yolks
2 tablespoons plus 1 teaspoon 00 flour (available at gourmet stores)
Pinch of kosher salt

Special equipment: Food mill

For the mushroom jus (makes about 5 cups):

5 black peppercorns
4 carrots, chopped
1 white onion, chopped
1 pound mushrooms
½ cup Madeira wine
4 cups vegetable stock

For serving:

1 tablespoon olive oil
2 pounds exotic mushrooms
¾ cup unsalted butter, divided
1 teaspoon chopped fresh thyme leaves
2 teaspoons chopped chives, divided
1 teaspoon lemon juice
½ cup raisins
1 tablespoon ice wine vinegar
6 large egg yolks
18 sorrel leaves
Raw mushroom, shaved (optional)

To prepare the potato gnocchi: Preheat oven to 400°F. Bake potatoes until tender, 45 to 60 minutes. Scoop out flesh and discard skin. Pass flesh through a food mill. While warm, stir in yolks, flour, and salt. Fold mixture twice, being careful not to overwork. Divide into 4 piles. Roll each into a long tube about 1 inch in diameter. Cut tubes into 1-inch sections to form gnocchi. Roll each gnocchi on the back of a fork to form ridges. Place on flour-dusted surface and allow to rest 10 minutes.

Bring a large pot of salted water to a simmer. Add gnocchi and cook until gnocchi float, about 10 seconds. Store, refrigerated, on a greased pan.

To prepare the mushroom jus: Combine all ingredients in a saucepan over low heat. Simmer for 45 minutes. Strain jus.

To serve: In a sauté pan over medium heat, heat olive oil. Sauté mushrooms until golden, 3 to 4 minutes. Add 6 tablespoons butter. When melted, add thyme and 1 teaspoon chives.

In a separate sauté pan over medium heat, heat remaining 6 tablespoons butter. Sauté prepared gnocchi until golden, about 2 minutes. Finish with remaining 1 teaspoon chives and lemon juice.

Soak raisins in ice wine vinegar until plump. Puree until smooth.

Divide mushrooms and gnocchi between six plates. Garnish each with raisin puree, egg yolk, sorrel leaves. Divide ¾ cup prepared mushroom jus between plates. Top each plate with shaved mushrooms, if using.

Melograno

RITTENHOUSE SQUARE
2012 SANSOM STREET
(215) 875-8116
WWW.MELOGRANORESTAURANT.COM

There is a formula for the Philadelphia BYOB: The wife runs the front of the house. The husband runs the kitchen. The hungry diners clog the sidewalk, clutching brown-bagged bottles of wine, waiting for a seat in the tiny no-reservations dining room.

When Melograno opened in 2003, it was just one of dozens of new BYOBs to employ this well-tested formula. Friendly and diplomatic Rosemarie Tran worked the hostess stand. Her Roman-born husband, Gianluca Demontis, cooked in the open kitchen. Would-be diners eyed the restaurant's thirty-four seats and its plates of handmade pastas hopefully.

It was those memorable pastas—pappardelle with truffled mushrooms and walnuts, roasted beet and mascarpone ravioli, traditional carbonara updated with a punch of anchovies—that first set Melograno apart in a town awash in Italian restaurants, BYOBs, and, especially, Italian BYOBs.

"I had worked in a lot of Italian restaurants," Demontis says. "But I wanted to bring the customers my food. Just rustic Italian dishes a little modernized."

With its success, Melograno changed the rules of the BYOB, moving to a space twice as large—but just as loud—as the intimate original and instituting a reservations policy, but you'll still find Tran greeting diners and Demontis tossing pastas.

CARBONARA AL PROFUMO DI TARTUFO BIANCO E ACCIUGHE

"One of my favorite foods is eggs, and the combination of eggs and fish has always worked for me," says Melograno chef-owner Gianluca Demontis. "At home I often make a frittata of anchovies, onions, and eggs. I thought it would make a great combination for carbonara, too. Carbonara has that salty element, so anchovies replace the pancetta in this recipe."

SERVES 4

8 salted anchovy fillets
3 large eggs plus 3 large egg yolks, lightly whisked
2 tablespoons white truffle paste or 1 tablespoon white truffle oil
4 tablespoons grated Parmesan cheese
1 tablespoon pistachios, cut in half

2 tablespoons extra-virgin olive oil
2 cloves garlic
14 ounces spaghetti
Sea salt and black pepper, as needed
4 fresh anchovy fillets

Rinse salted anchovy fillets and remove central bone. In a large bowl, mash salted anchovies with a fork. Add eggs and truffle paste or truffle oil and mix gently. Add cheese and pistachios.

In a large sauté pan over medium heat, heat olive oil. Add garlic and cook until browned. Discard garlic. Remove pan from heat.

In a large saucepan over high heat, bring salted water to a boil. Cook spaghetti to al dente according to package instructions. Drain pasta and add to hot oil. Add egg mixture and cook over low heat, mixing constantly, for 1 minute. Season with salt and pepper. Divide between four plates and top each with a fresh anchovy fillet.

Testaroli al Pesto di Asparagi

"The *testaroli* is an ancient recipe that I found in a history book about medieval life and costume in the Tuscan and Ligurian region when I was in Italy," says Melograno chef-owner Gianluca Demontis. "I like this type of pasta because it really absorb sauces."

SERVES 4

2 pounds asparagus
4 cups 00 flour (available at gourmet stores)
4 cups warm water
1 teaspoon sea salt
1 cup almonds, toasted
3 cloves garlic
1 cup olive oil
3 cups basil leaves
1 cup plus 2 tablespoons grated Parmesan
   cheese, divided
½ cup plus 2 tablespoons grated Pecorino
   Romano cheese, divided
Additional sea salt and black pepper, as needed
Vegetable oil, as needed
Extra-virgin olive oil, as needed

Over high heat, bring a large saucepan of water to a boil. Blanch asparagus for 2 to 3 minutes. Remove asparagus and plunge into ice water to stop cooking.

In a bowl, combine flour and water gradually until the consistency of thin pancake batter. Add salt and strain into another bowl. Rest crepe (testaroli) batter for 30 minutes.

In a food processor, combine blanched asparagus, almonds, garlic, and olive oil. Process until well combined. Rest 1 minute, add basil, 1 cup Parmesan, and ½ cup Pecorino Romano, and process until combined to form pesto. Season with salt and pepper.

Lightly coat a crepe pan or sauté pan with vegetable oil. Heat pan over medium heat. Ladle 6 tablespoons of batter into the hot pan, moving ladle in a circular motion over the batter to create a thin, round disc. When the center of the crepe starts to brown, about 30 seconds, flip crepe and cook an additional 15 seconds. Transfer crepe to clean kitchen towel. Repeat with remaining batter to make about 16 crepes.

Cut crepes into bite-size pieces. In a saucepan over medium heat, combine crepe and pesto. Add hot water if pesto is too thick. Cook until warmed. Divide between four plates and top with remaining 2 tablespoons Parmesan, 2 tablespoons Pecorino Romano, and extra-virgin olive oil.

HAN DYNASTY

OLD CITY
108 CHESTNUT STREET
(215) 922-1888
WWW.HANDYNASTY.NET

Han Chiang is known among Philadelphia diners for two things: his menu of fiery Szechuan dishes and his insistence that you order what he tells you, with the occasional expletive attached to the command. It's all part of the show that has made Chiang's mini-empire of Dynasties (Exton, Royersford, Old City) a foodie phenomenon.

"Yes, I tell my customer what to eat," says Chiang. "They will place an order, and I will change it for them. They don't know."

There, Chiang has a point. Most Philadelphia diners don't know the traditional Szechuan dishes Chiang takes pride in—three-cup chicken, lion's head meatballs, green bean noodle. They know, to quote the chef, "their crappy Chinese takeout."

"I would rather eat old hot dogs at a 7-Eleven than Americanized Chinese food," Taiwanese-born Chiang says, loudly.

Chiang is known for giving wayward diners just one choice—"Do you like spicy or not spicy?"—but with Chiang's Szechuan menu it's really just a question of spicy or spicier.

At his original suburban location, Chiang grudgingly admits, he serves General Tso's and beef and broccoli alongside the chili oil–spiked classics he evangelizes for. In Old City, Chiang makes no such compromises, and the twenty-course Szechuan banquet he hosts the first Monday night of each month is the hottest ticket in town. "There's so much good Chinese food out there," Chiang says, "but nobody has the guts to do it here. We need to let Americans know what Chinese food is really about."

DAN DAN NOODLES

"The long pole that you carry across your shoulder with a basket on either side—that is called *dan*. Dan Dan Noodles were sold from the baskets with sauce and you mixed it yourself," says Han Dynasty chef-owner Han Chiang. "At the restaurant, I make my own soy sauce and my own chili oil, but even if you don't, this dish is full of flavor. People get addicted to it."

SERVES 4

2½ tablespoons vegetable oil, divided
2 ounces ground pork
½ tablespoon minced garlic
2 tablespoons preserved Chinese vegetables
    (available at Asian markets)
1/3 cup plus ½ tablespoon soy sauce, divided
2 tablespoons sesame paste
2 tablespoons water

2 tablespoons chili oil
½ tablespoon Szechuan peppercorn oil (available
    at Asian markets)
2½ tablespoons granulated sugar
1 pound flour noodles

Special equipment: Wok

In a wok over high heat, heat ½ tablespoon vegetable oil. Brown pork and garlic. Add preserved vegetables and ½ tablespoon soy sauce. Remove from heat.

In a bowl, whisk together remaining 2 tablespoons vegetable oil and sesame paste until emulsified. Add remaining ⅓ cup soy sauce, water, chili oil, peppercorn oil, and sugar and whisk until emulsified.

Cook flour noodles according to package instructions.

Pour sauce into an empty serving bowl, add cooked noodles, and top with ground pork. Toss tableside.

Modo Mio

NORTHERN LIBERTIES
161 WEST GIRARD AVENUE
(215) 203-8707

Chef Peter McAndrews knew he wanted to do Italian food his way. "Italian food is my favorite, but I don't like Italian restaurants. Those are things to make at home, not in a restaurant," he says. Instead of the standards, you'll find dishes like chicken liver bruschetta and veal and rabbit ravioli on the menu at his miniature Northern Liberties BYOB. "I like people to take a chance," he says.

In many ways, Modo Mio was taking a chance. This stretch of Girard Avenue is quiet; the storefront, unassuming. McAndrews was adamant about wanting to do his food—chicken and salmon, no; offal, yes—his way, which meant small European-style portions and multiple courses. But that chance paid off: The city's foodies quickly discovered this reasonably priced *menu turista:* a self-designed four-course tasting menu, ending with a complimentary shot of Sambuca.

Open the door to that unassuming storefront and you feel as though you've found the city's best dinner party, a crowded room of happy chatter and clinking glassware. "I think we've had three slow nights in four years," McAndrews says.

McAndrews estimates he's created four hundred different dishes for the menu in the first four years. His favorite: grilled lamb shanks garnished with *cervella.* Don't ask for the translation. Just enjoy.

Bucatini Amatriciana

"*Modo mio* means 'my way,' and this is my take on Italian food," Modo Mio chef-owner Peter McAndrews says. "But the pastas I keep classic. The Italians can do no wrong with pasta. Everything else can do with a little bit of this or a little bit of that, but the pasta is perfect. Cook it low and slow. That's the Italian way, just let it go. Have some wine, have some fun."

SERVES 4

½ cup olive oil, divided
½ cup diced pancetta
1 large Spanish onion, diced
1 teaspoon red pepper flakes
2 28-ounce cans whole plum tomatoes with juice
Kosher salt, as needed
1 pound dried bucatini
2 tablespoons chopped flat-leaf parsley
½ cup grated Pecorino Romano cheese

In a large sauté pan over medium-low heat, heat ¼ cup olive oil and slowly cook pancetta and onion until lightly browned, 10 to 15 minutes. Add red pepper flakes and cook 1 minute. Hand-crush plum tomatoes and add to sauté pan. Season with salt.

Bring a large pot of salted water to a boil over high heat. Cook pasta in boiling water according to package instructions. When al dente, drain pasta, reserving 1 cup cooking liquid, and transfer pasta to sauté pan. Add pasta water as necessary to form light sauce. Add remaining ¼ cup olive oil, parsley, and cheese. Cook 1 to 2 minutes, tossing until pasta is evenly coated with sauce.

Bombolini il Pazzo
{The Farmers' Cabinet}

"I feel that vermouth is an unsung and underrated ingredient in cocktails," says bartender Phoebe Esmon. "Good vermouth is hard to beat. I've been known to put it into my pasta sauce upon occasion!"

SERVES 1

1½ ounces Dolin sweet vermouth
¾ ounce Dolin dry vermouth
¾ ounce Averna amaro
2 drops orange flower water
Ice
Orange peel

Special equipment: Lighter

Stir vermouths, amaro, and orange water over ice until well chilled. Strain into a chilled cocktail glass. Cut an orange disk, including some pith (unlike in a twist), from the peel. Hold the disk above the drink. Heat the orange side with a lighter and squeeze disk to release orange oils.

1113 Walnut Street
(215) 923-1113
www.thefarmerscabinet.com

ENTREES

Whatever you are craving, you'll find it in Philadelphia. There's Italian and French, of course, but also Mexican and Israeli, Southern and Spanish, Indian and English, Portuguese and Japanese. And then there's the beloved Philadelphia gastropub, a culinary update on the city's corner bars, where some of Philly's most talented chefs have turned their attention to the roast chicken and burger basics.

These restaurants—and the recipes here—have one important thing in common: They are personal projects, an expression of a chef's culinary identity. Whether a dish had its start in a well-worn family cookbook or was a classic preparation, it has been shaped into something new by the chef's experiences, the region's ingredients, and the Philadelphia diners' expectations.

When cooking at home, the charge is the same. Start with your favorite restaurant's recipe, absorb the cooking wisdom of the city's top chefs—and then cook a dish to meet your own tastes.

Pub & Kitchen

GRADUATE HOSPITAL
1946 LOMBARD STREET
(215) 545-0350
WWW.THEPUBANDKITCHEN.COM

Ed Hackett and Jonathan Adams (pictured below) are refugees from fine dining. The pair—the driving force in Pub & Kitchen's dining room and kitchen, respectively—did their time in the dining rooms and kitchens of the city's white tablecloth restaurants before opening Pub & Kitchen with owner Dan Clark.

"We both got a little burned out from fine dining," Adams says. He pauses: "This is even harder than fine dining."

That's because Pub & Kitchen isn't trying to surprise you as Adams did during his time at now-defunct Snackbar. (Think miso-glazed apples crusted with wasabi peas.) The goal here is comfortable and familiar: roast chicken, burgers, fish-and-chips. "It's honest, no tricks, no hidden agenda," says Adams. "The food is very transparent. There's nothing to hide behind."

At the bar and in the dining room—and in warmer months, spilling out onto the sidewalk—the restaurant is a hodgepodge of Phillies fans and first dates, solo diners and family dinners. "It's the *Cheers* mentality," says Adams. "We want the mailman and the dancer and the mayor."

And the chefs: Stop by after the dinner rush and you are likely to find the city's chefs and servers gathering at Pub & Kitchen's long bar for a late-night burger and beer, perhaps the best endorsement a restaurant can get.

Roasted Chicken with Mustard Green Beans & Irish Soda Biscuits

"Cooking is a legacy," says Pub & Kitchen chef Jonathan Adams. "And Sunday dinner is a family tradition. These biscuits are adapted from a recipe my grandmother would make, and the cast-iron pan in the picture is from my wife's grandfather, who had it for fifty years."
(Note: Chicken must be brined overnight.)

SERVES 4

For the biscuits (makes 12 biscuits):

1⅔ cups buttermilk
½ cup whiskey
4¾ cups all-purpose flour
⅓ cup brown sugar
½ tablespoon kosher salt
¾ tablespoon baking soda
¼ cup chopped chives
2 tablespoons chopped flat-leaf parsley
7¾ tablespoons cold butter, diced

Special equipment: Pastry cutter

For the chicken:

1 whole 3½-pound chicken
2 cups pale ale
1 cup water
½ cup kosher salt
1 bay leaf
1 tablespoon black peppercorns
16–20 sprigs thyme, divided
1 Spanish onion, cut in half
1 head garlic
Flaky salt and black pepper, as needed

Special equipment: Meat thermometer

For the green beans:

½ pound green beans
2 tablespoons unsalted butter
1 shallot, diced
Kosher salt and black pepper, as needed
2 tablespoons whole-grain mustard
¼ cup beer or water
Lemon juice, as needed

To prepare the biscuits: Preheat oven to 375°F. Lightly grease a nonstick muffin pan. In a bowl, combine buttermilk and whiskey and set aside. In a separate large bowl, combine flour, sugar, salt, baking soda, chives, and parsley. Cut diced butter into the flour mixture using a pastry cutter. Once the butter is thoroughly mixed with the flour mixture, fold in buttermilk and whiskey gently, until just combined. Cover and allow to rest at room temperature for 30 minutes. (Biscuits can be prepared to this point up to 1 day in advance.) Spoon biscuit dough into muffin molds and bake until golden brown, 12 to 15 minutes.

To prepare the chicken: Rinse chicken with cold water and pat dry. In a saucepan over high heat, combine pale ale, water, salt, bay leaf, black peppercorns, and half of the thyme. Bring to a boil, whisking until salt has dissolved. Remove brine from heat and transfer to a container large enough to hold brine and chicken. Allow brine to cool to room temperature. Submerge chicken completely and brine, refrigerated, overnight.

Preheat oven to 400°F. Remove chicken from brine and rinse with cold water to remove herbs and peppercorns. Dry chicken, inside and out, and allow to come to room temperature. Stuff the cavity with onion, garlic, and remaining thyme. Season outside of chicken generously with salt and pepper.

Truss chicken. (See "Step by Step," at right.) Place in a roasting pan and place pan on the middle rack of the oven. Roast in preheated oven until chicken has started to brown, about 15 minutes. Turn heat down to 350°F and continue cooking until a meat thermometer inserted in the thickest part of the thigh reads 155°F, about 30 minutes. (Cover chicken with aluminum foil if it begins to brown too much.) Remove chicken from the oven, reserving pan juices. The internal temperature will continue to rise as the chicken rests. Rest, covered, for 30 minutes before carving. Over high heat, reduce pan juices by half, skimming fat as needed.

To prepare the green beans: Bring a large saucepan of heavily salted water to a boil over high heat. Add green beans and blanch at a rolling boil until just tender, 4 to 5 minutes. Shock in an ice bath. Drain beans and allow beans to dry.

In a large sauté pan over medium heat, melt butter. When butter begins to foam, add shallots, season lightly with salt and pepper, and cook until translucent, 2 to 3 minutes. Add green beans and toss with shallots and butter until well coated and warmed through, about 3 minutes. Raise heat to high and add mustard and beer or water. Season green beans with salt, pepper, and lemon juice. Remove from heat and drain on a paper towel before serving.

To serve: Place green beans on a platter and top with carved chicken. Pour pan juices over chicken. Serve with warm biscuits.

STEP BY STEP: TRUSSING A CHICKEN

"The point of all of this: Tucking the wings prevents them from burning and pushes the breast meat upwards," says Pub & Kitchen chef Jonathan Adams.

1. TUCK

Lay the chicken breast side up on a cutting board. Tuck the wing tips behind the joint where the wing meets the breast. To personify, imagine the bird hanging out on a couch, with its "hands" behind its "head."

2. TIE

Cut 18 inches of butcher twine. Center the twine behind the upper back of the chicken and pull both ends around the wings and along the breast line on either side inside the thigh. Cross the legs above the twine and tie a knot around the ankles.

3. ROAST

Follow your favorite recipe. Trussing the bird keeps it compact and shields the breast from excess heat.

New York Strip Steak with Confit Potatoes & Asparagus

"Timing is essential for this recipe," says Pub & Kitchen chef Jonathan Adams. "Sear and baste the meat, then allow forty-five minutes for the sauce. Finishing the steak in the oven will get the meat hot again. The long rest time is good for the meat."

SERVES 4

For the shallots:

¼ cup unsalted butter
12 shallots
2 sprigs thyme
½ cup soy sauce
½ cup Worcestershire sauce
½ cup low-sodium beef broth

For the potato confit:

3 pounds fingerling potatoes, scrubbed
5 pounds rendered duck fat

For the steak and sauce:

4 12-ounce New York strip steaks,
    trimmed of fat
Kosher salt and black pepper
½ cup grape seed oil
½ cup unsalted butter
4 garlic cloves, crushed, divided
6 sprigs thyme, divided
2 ribs celery, diced
1 carrot, diced
1 onion, diced
1 750-milliliter bottle dry red wine
1½ cups low-sodium beef broth
1 cup veal demi-glace (available at
    gourmet markets)
1 fresh bay leaf

For serving:

Flaky sea salt, as needed
2 pounds asparagus, trimmed and sliced
    on the bias into ½-inch pieces

To prepare the shallots: In a sauté pan over low heat, melt butter. Add shallots and cook until they start to brown. Increase heat to medium-high. Add thyme, soy sauce, Worcestershire sauce, and beef broth. Cook uncovered until shallots are soft and liquid is syrupy, about 20 minutes. Shallots can be made up to 2 days in advance. They will develop a deeper flavor with time. Store in liquid until use.

To prepare the potato confit: Preheat oven to 325°F.

Place potatoes in a deep casserole dish. Cover with duck fat. Cover with aluminum foil and cook until a skewer inserted in a potato comes out clean, without resistance, about 90 minutes. Allow potatoes to cool in fat to room temperature. Strain, reserving potatoes and fat. Slice potatoes lengthwise. (Reserve fat for future use.)

To prepare the steak and sauce: Let steak come to room temperature and season with salt and pepper. Preheat a large cast-iron pan over medium heat. Add oil and heat until oil begins to shimmer and moves fluidly in the pan. Add steaks and cook 4 minutes. Flip steaks and cook 2 more minutes. Add butter, 2 cloves garlic, and 2 sprigs thyme. Turn heat to low. As the butter melts and

starts to brown, baste steak by spooning butter over steak repeatedly for 2 to 3 minutes. Remove steaks to a wire rack and cover meat with foil. Allow meat to rest.

Use the same cast-iron pan to prepare the sauce. Pour off excess butter and reheat pan over medium-high heat. Add celery, carrots, onion, and remaining 2 cloves garlic and sauté until they just start to caramelize. Add red wine and increase heat to high. Reduce until about ¾ cup wine remains. Add beef broth, demi-glace, bay leaf, and remaining 4 sprigs thyme. Bring to a boil. Transfer sauce to a saucepan.

Over low heat, simmer sauce, uncovered, for 30 to 40 minutes. Skim off fat or foam that rises to the surface. When the sauce has reduced and thickly coats the back of a spoon, strain.

To serve: Preheat oven to 325°F. Warm steaks in oven for 8 minutes. Slice steak and divide between four plates. Top with sauce. Garnish with sea salt.

In a sauté pan over medium-high heat, sauté potato confit, cut side down, for 3 minutes. Add asparagus and cook for an additional 2 minutes. Add shallots. Serve alongside steak.

OSTERIA

NORTH PHILLY
640 NORTH BROAD STREET
(215) 763-0920
WWW.OSTERIAPHILLY.COM

Philadelphia waited nine years. For those nine years, Marc Vetri stayed in the kitchen of his namesake Spruce Street restaurant (page 76), cooking the city's most lauded meals for the lucky few who scored a reservation in the intimate dining room and turning down all offers to open a second spot. (Meanwhile, in those nine years, restaurateur Stephen Starr opened seventeen spots.)

Then, finally, there was Osteria.

That Vetri's sequel opened in a former factory building on a quiet stretch of North Broad

Street was a surprise. That Vetri—along with longtime business partner Jeff Benjamin and protégé and partner Jeffrey Michaud— quickly made this North Philly address a dining destination was not.

The partners use words like "casual" and "rustic" to describe the restaurant, and it is. It is convivial to Vetri's hush. It is pizzas and pastas to Vetri's twelve-course tasting menu. It is more than a hundred seats and a first-come-first-served bar to Vetri's thirty-five seats and always-filled reservation book.

But there's nothing casual about the commitment in the open kitchen, where James Beard award–winner Michaud turns out crisp-crusted pizzas topped with house-cured cotechino sausage, wild boar Bolognese with handmade pastas, and pork Milanese inspired by his Italian mother-in-law.

Pork Milanese with Arugula Salad

"My Italian mother-in-law makes this dish the classic way with veal. My wife makes it with chicken. We have a great pig farmer, so I tried it with pork," says Osteria chef-owner Jeffery Michaud. "Other than that, this recipe is exactly the way I've had it in Milan. It's a classic that doesn't need to be changed."

SERVES 4

4 6-ounce bone-in pork chops
Kosher salt and black pepper, as needed
6 large eggs
2 cups bread crumbs
Unsalted butter, as needed
1¼ cups olive oil, plus additional olive oil
     as needed
¼ cup lemon juice
3 cups arugula
1 lemon, sliced
½ cup shaved Parmesan cheese
Kosher salt and black pepper, as needed

Pound the pork chops with a meat mallet until about ½-inch thick. Season meat on both sides with salt and pepper. In a bowl large enough to fit a pork chop, whisk eggs. Place bread crumbs in another large bowl. Coat pork chops with egg, then bread crumbs.

In a sauté pan over medium heat, combine equal parts butter and olive oil. When butter is melted, there should be ⅛ inch of the butter-oil mixture. Cook pork chops until golden brown, 3 to 4 minutes on each side. Drain on paper towels. Season again with salt and pepper.

To assemble the salad, whisk together 1¼ cups olive oil and lemon juice. Toss with arugula. Season with salt and pepper

Divide pork chops between four plates. Top with arugula salad and garnish with lemon slices and cheese.

El Rey

Rittenhouse Square
2013 Chestnut Street
(215) 563-3330
www.elreyrestaurant.com

"This place was a dive," restaurateur Stephen Starr says of the Chestnut Street space that became El Rey. "That's why I liked it."

When Starr revamped the Midtown IV Diner into a "left-of-center" Mexican joint, he didn't want to lose that vibe. The restaurateur, long known for his polished, stage-set-perfect restaurants, wanted a touch of off-kilter authenticity for El Rey. For Starr, that meant keeping the Formica, Naugahyde, and faux stone and adding velvet Elvises and an obscure rockabilly soundtrack. (An attached bar, with its entrance on alley-like Ranstead Street, was even more of a dive. No more—Starr completely overhauled that portion of the building, creating the Ranstead Room, a dim, moody cocktail den.) A sign above the door announces, "*Esto cambiara su vida*"—"This will change your life."

Chef Dionicio Jimenez, who began his Philadelphia restaurant career as a dishwasher at Vetri and went on to earn rave reviews as the chef at Old City Mexican Xochitl, was tasked with creating a menu of traditional Mexican flavors inspired by his native Puebla, a charge which ensured that the new restaurant didn't compete with Starr's more mainstream Mexican restaurant El Vez, inspired by frozen blood-orange margaritas by the pitcher and a bicycle-turned-guacamole cart.

In this wacky environment, Jimenez serves up homey dishes like nopales (cactus), *esquites* (warm corn salad), and complex moles—and nachos piled high with black beans and chorizo, cheese and salsa, a must-have at any authentically *Philadelphian* Mexican restaurant.

CHILE EN NOGADA

"This recipe comes from Puebla. It is a really traditional dish in July and August when the peppers have a little more heat and especially in September," says El Rey chef Dionicio Jimenez. "September 16 is Mexican Independence Day, and Chile en Nogada—the parsley, pomegranate, and walnuts—represents the Mexican flag."

SERVES 6

4 tablespoons vegetable oil, divided
1 Spanish onion, chopped
2 cloves garlic, minced
½ cup diced dried apricot
½ cup diced dried pineapple
½ cup diced dried papaya
½ cup golden raisins
2 bay leaves
1 cinnamon stick
1 pound ground beef
Kosher salt and black pepper, as needed
1 cup toasted slivered almonds
4 ounces cream cheese
1 cup whole milk
1 cup chopped walnuts, divided
6 poblano peppers
$^1/_3$ cup chopped flat-leaf parsley
1 pomegranate, seeds only

Preheat oven to 350°F.

In a sauté pan over medium heat, heat 3 tablespoons oil. Sauté onion and garlic until transparent. Add dried fruit, bay leaves, and cinnamon and sauté until warmed through, 2 to 3 minutes. Add ground beef and sauté until cooked through, 5 to 10 minutes. Season with salt and pepper. Stir in almonds. Remove from heat and allow to cool. Remove bay leaves and cinnamon.

In a blender, combine cream cheese, milk, and $^2/_3$ cup walnuts. Season with salt and pepper. Blend until nogada sauce is smooth and creamy.

Place poblano peppers on a baking sheet and drizzle with remaining 1 tablespoon vegetable oil. Roast until skin comes off easily, 3 to 5 minutes. Use a clean dish towel to wipe skin off peppers. Cut a slit along the side of each pepper. Remove seeds and stuff with cooled beef mixture. Top stuffed peppers with nogada sauce. Garnish with parsley, pomegranate seeds, and remaining $^1/_3$ cup walnuts in bands from left to right to resemble the Mexican flag.

PHILADELPHIA ICON: CHEESESTEAK

Humphrey Bogart, Oprah Winfrey, Bobby Flay, Kevin Bacon, and, of course, Sylvester Stallone—they have all paid homage to the Philadelphia cheesesteak. Forget the lightning rod and the Constitution, this simple sandwich with a slang all its own is Philly's best-known invention and our best ambassador.

The history of the cheesesteak starts at a hot dog cart in South Philly around 1930, when the owner, Pat, sold his own lunch of steak and onions on a roll to a hungry cabbie, and a Philadelphia icon was born.

But it was more than a decade before cheese and steak became one word. Again, Pat's King of Steaks gets the credit. Provolone was the original. Later Whiz would become the true king of steaks.

The 1960s brought Jim's and Geno's and those signed celebrity photos. Then came Steve's, Tony Luke's, Rick's, the obligatory politician photo ops (remember John Kerry and the Swiss cheese scandal?), the blessedly short-lived McCheesesteak, and the ongoing Philly argument: Who makes city's best cheesesteak?

There are more than a thousand contenders for that title. Even the city's top restaurants entered the fray with cheesesteak empanadas (Good Dog Bar, page 124), Chinese cheesesteak buns (Sampan, page 6), cheesesteak fries (Village Whiskey, page 153)—and the much-talked-about, less-ordered one hundred-dollar version at Barclay Prime, which added Waygu beef, taleggio, and *foie gras* to the city's "whiz wit" lexicon.

ZAHAV

SOCIETY HILL
237 ST. JAMES PLACE
(215) 625-8800
WWW.ZAHAVRESTAURANT.COM

Chef-owner Michael Solomonov (pictured below) struggles with how to define Zahav, his exuberant Society Hill restaurant: "I guess most people would call it modern Israeli. The irony is, there's nothing like this is Israel." Instead, the chef borrows from Israel's exotic pantry—filled with flavors from each culture that has called the region home—to create dishes that might more properly be called "modern Solomonov."

This is Israel through the eyes of an Israeli-born, Pittsburgh-raised, James Beard award–winning chef with an affection for culinary history and Korean fried chicken (the latter indulged by his more recent project, Federal Donuts). That Solo—as he is widely known—is cooking for an audience that may have never heard of *labneh,* kibbe, or *mujadara* hasn't dampened his enthusiasm or the restaurant's popularity: "Ten years ago, there wouldn't have been a Zahav, but people are more willing to try things now. We go through fifteen pounds of duck hearts a week." (Grilled with a carrot-turnip salad and onion puree.)

Solomonov and his business partner Steve Cook are also behind the Hill Country BBQ at Percy Street Barbecue (page 20), but you'll most often find the chef in the kitchen at Zahav, plating traditional hummus (four types, including a warm, buttery Turkish version) and *laffa* hot from the *taboon,* and should-be traditional dishes like beef cheeks cured in an Ethiopian spice mix and braised in Turkish coffee.

Chicken Freekeh

"I always start with the ingredient here and pick a culture there," says Zahav chef-owner Michael Solomonov. "This is a pretty simple rice pilaf with Amish chicken and flavors from Jordan and Egypt. The secret is the cinnamon."

SERVES 4

2 cups chicken stock
1 teaspoon black peppercorns
3 sprigs cilantro, stems and leaves separated
2 sticks cinnamon
2 boneless, skinless chicken breasts
Kosher salt and black pepper, as needed
2 tablespoons chicken fat or olive oil
2 tablespoons diced Spanish onion
$2/3$ cup freekeh (available at Middle Eastern markets)
4 tablespoon toasted slivered almonds

In a large saucepan over medium heat, bring chicken stock with peppercorns, cilantro stems, and cinnamon to a simmer. Season chicken breasts with salt and poach in simmering broth until cooked through, approximately 15 minutes. Remove the chicken and keep warm. Strain and reserve broth.

Warm chicken fat or olive oil in a medium sauté pan over medium heat. Add onion and cook until translucent, approximately 5 minutes. Season with salt. Add freekeh and cook over medium heat until the freekeh is fragrant and well-coated with the chicken fat or olive oil. Add half of reserved broth and continue to cook over medium heat, stirring constantly, until the liquid is fully absorbed. Repeat with remaining broth and cook until freekeh is al dente but not dry. Using two forks, shred chicken and fold into the freekeh, with toasted almonds and cilantro leaves. Season with salt and pepper.

WHOLE ROASTED LAMB SHOULDER WITH POMEGRANATE

"This was the first thing we ever made at Zahav. When it was still under construction, we had a seder at the restaurant," says Zahav chef-owner Michael Solomonov. "I had lamb shoulder around, and lamb and pomegranate are a classic. When we tried it, it was, 'Dude, we have to have this on the menu.'"
(Note: Lamb shoulder must be marinated for 2 days. Chickpeas must be soaked overnight.)

SERVES 4

For the brine:

3 gallons water
6 cups kosher salt
1½ cups granulated sugar
1 pound garlic bulbs, bulbs cut in half
½ cup whole allspice
½ cup black peppercorns
½ cup fennel seeds
12 stems parsley
12 stems savory

For the lamb shoulder:

1 bone-in lamb shoulder (about 6 pounds)
4 cups dried chickpeas
1 teaspoon baking soda
4 cups pomegranate juice
4 cups water
2 sprigs mint
¼ cup flat-leaf parsley, roughly chopped

Special equipment: **Charcoal grill**

To prepare the brine: Combine all ingredients for the brine in a large saucepan over high heat. Bring to a boil. Remove from heat. Chill thoroughly before using.

To prepare the lamb shoulder: Using a fork, puncture lamb shoulder on all sides. Submerge lamb in brine for 48 hours, using a weight if necessary to keep lamb completely submerged.

Soak chickpeas in water with baking soda overnight.

Prepare a charcoal fire. Remove lamb from brine and pat dry. Grill lamb over indirect heat for about 45 minutes, being careful to avoid flare-ups from dripping fat.

Preheat oven to 350°F. Remove lamb from grill and place in a deep roasting pan. Drain chickpeas and rinse in cold water. Add chickpeas and pomegranate juice to roasting pan. Add water to just cover lamb. Cover roasting pan with a double layer of aluminum foil and place in oven. Braise lamb, basting meat with braising liquid once each hour until meat easily separates from the bone, about 5 hours.

Remove from oven and allow lamb to rest in braising liquid for 1 hour. Remove lamb from roasting pan and transfer braising liquid to a large saucepan. Simmer liquid over medium-high heat, skimming regularly to remove fat. When the braising liquid coats the back of a spoon and is reduced to about 4 cups, remove from heat. Add mint and parsley.

Preheat oven to 450°F. Return lamb to roasting pan and top with 1 cup braising liquid. Roast lamb until caramelized, about 5 minutes.

To serve: Remove lamb to a warm platter. Spoon reduced braising liquid and chickpeas on top of lamb. Serve immediately.

AMADA

OLD CITY
217–219 CHESTNUT STREET
(215) 625-2450
WWW.AMADARESTAURANT.COM

Amada was Philadelphia's first taste of what was to come from chef-turned-restaurateur Jose Garces (pictured right). Later there would be the rapid-fire opening of other Philadelphia favorites (Distrito, page 10, Village Whiskey, page 153, and Guapos Tacos, page 151, to name just a few), the James Beard award, and *The Next Iron Chef* victory, but first there was *tortilla Española* with saffron aioli, *piquillos rellenos* stuffed with tender crab, tender calamari seared *a la plancha,* and spicy *patatas bravas,* a luxe version of the equally addictive Tater Tot.

Amada, which opened in 2005, was the restaurant Garces had wanted to open since his days in culinary school, when he wrote a strikingly similar business plan for a class: a Spanish tapas restaurant that captured both traditional Iberian flavors—serrano ham, manchego, chorizo, spiked with olives, vinegars, citrus—and the vibe of the country's tapas bars. In Barcelona, *tapeo* is more than a culinary phenomenon; it's also a cultural one. In those crowded environs, tapas is as much about conversation as it is about *charcuteria.*

Garces's dream restaurant took on more details during a stint cooking in Andalusia, Spain. "The sangria barrels behind the bar, the hanging hams, the charcuterie slicer—all those elements transport me back to my days in Spain," says Garces, mentally walking through the stylish, evocative dining rooms.

"I want to transport Philadelphians. I want to give them a true, authentic Spanish experience, to give them that true festive feel of Spain," says Garces.

Paella Valenciana

"Start to finish the cook makes the paella at Amada to order," says Amada chef-owner Jose Garces. "I want it to be an authentic food experience for our customer. There are a few things here you wouldn't see in Spain, like the herb salad on top of the paella. It's not traditional, but it cuts the richness and gives the dish a freshness."

SERVES 2

3½ cups chicken broth
Pinch of saffron
Kosher salt and black pepper, as needed
1¼ cups diced Spanish onion, divided
4 tablespoons extra-virgin olive oil, divided
2 tablespoons unsalted butter
1½ cups bomba rice
½ cup frozen peas
¼ cup julienned piquillo peppers
3 ounces chorizo, diced
10 mussels
8 cherrystone clams or cockles
5 shrimp
2 tablespoons julienned black olives
2 tablespoons chopped flat-leaf parsley,
    plus ¼ cup whole flat-leaf parsley leaves
1 large shallot, minced
2 tablespoons lemon juice
1 teaspoon granulated sugar
¼ cup cherry tomatoes, cut in half
1 boneless, skinless chicken breast
1 lemon, cut into wedges

Preheat oven to 350°F.

In a saucepan over high heat, bring chicken broth to a boil. Add pinch of saffron and season with salt. Reduce heat and simmer until reduced to 1½ cups, about 30 minutes.

In a paella pan or large cast-iron pan over medium-high heat, sauté 1 cup onion in 2 tablespoons olive oil and butter. In a large bowl, combine rice, saffron chicken broth, peas, piquillo peppers, chorizo, mussels, clams or cockles, shrimp, black olives, and chopped parsley. Season with salt. Transfer mixture to pan. Bring to a boil and remove from heat. Cover tightly with aluminum foil and cook in the oven for 25 minutes.

To prepare a vinaigrette, combine shallot, lemon juice, olive oil, and sugar and whisk until sugar is dissolved. Season with salt and pepper. In a small bowl, combine whole parsley leaves, tomatoes, and remaining ¼ cup onion. Toss with vinaigrette. Place salad on top of paella.

Sear or grill chicken breast until cooked through. Slice and place on top of paella. Squeeze 2 lemon wedges over paella. Garnish with remaining lemon wedges.

Good Dog Bar

Rittenhouse Square
224 South 15th Street
(215) 985-9600
www.gooddogbar.com

Chef Jessica O'Donnell did her time in the city's fine dining kitchens, but she's made her mark at dive bar-turned-gastropub Good Dog Bar. The crowded, dark bar, as proud of its vintage Ms. Pac-Man machine as its beer list (everything from Ommegang to PBR pounders), boasts a menu of pork belly with pickled watermelon, chicken fingers cordon bleu, and duck pot pie. But it is the burger—a burger so memorable that *Philadelphia Inquirer* food critic Craig LaBan wrote a song about it—that has earned O'Donnell her place in Philadelphia culinary lore.

The secret to the Good Dog burger: Hidden within the hulking half-pound burger is a pungent core of molten blue cheese.

"Our goal was to have the best burger in Philly, but I don't remember exactly how the Good Dog burger came together," says O'Donnell. "Since we opened, I've seen a lot of recipes that put cheddar in the burger, but the blue cheese is much better because it melts so well and really cooks in with the meat."

O'Donnell estimates that the kitchen turns out an average of six hundred burgers a week. The Good Dog burger record is 952 burgers in one week—that's nearly five hundred pounds of beef and sixty pounds of cheese.

Roquefort-Stuffed Burger

"The biggest thing when you are cooking this burger is to get the grill good and hot. Just put the lid down and let it heat," says Good Dog Bar chef Jessica O'Donnell. "Then put the burger on the counter and pound it to an inch thick, uniform all around so it will cook evenly."

SERVES 4

1 tablespoon unsalted butter
1 tablespoon olive oil
2 Spanish onions, sliced thin
Kosher salt and black pepper, as needed
1 tablespoon chopped fresh thyme leaves
2 pounds 80 percent lean ground beef
4 ounces Roquefort cheese, cut into 4 pieces
4 brioche rolls, sliced in half and lightly toasted

Special equipment: Grill

In a sauté pan over medium-high heat, combine butter and olive oil. Season onion with salt and pepper. When butter is melted in the pan, add onions, stirring to coat onions with oil. Let sit until onions start to brown, about 20 minutes. Stir again and add thyme. Reduce heat to low and simmer until liquid released by onions is almost dry and onions are caramelized.

Preheat grill to high. Roll ground beef into 4 loose balls. Pat balls into flat patties and place a piece of cheese in the center of each. Fold the edges of each patty up around the cheese and roll back into a ball with cheese in the center. Gently flatten each ball into a patty about 1-inch thick. Season both sides generously with salt and pepper. Grill to medium, about 6 minutes on each side. Place burger on bottom half of bun, top with caramelized onions and top of bun.

Koo Zee Doo

NORTHERN LIBERTIES
614 NORTH 2ND STREET
(215) 923-8080
WWW.KOOZEEDOO.COM

Most chefs would have been nervous about serving chicken gizzards to the average Philadelphia diner, but that wasn't what had chef David Gilberg worried when he opened Koo Zee Doo with his wife, pastry chef Carla Gonçalves. "We were nervous about Philadelphia's Portuguese community," says the chef, striving for an authenticity in his homey Portuguese classics.

But those tender white wine–braised gizzards and his other rustic, family-style dishes were an instant hit. "They may come in very skeptical," Gilberg says of his toughest critics, "but they usually leave pleased."

One of the few Portuguese restaurants in the city—and the only one to cater to the wine-toting foodie crowd—Koo Zee Doo is often a diner's first introduction to the flavors of Portugal. They were new to Gilberg, too, when he first met his future wife and spent Sunday dinners in her mother's kitchen: "Salt cod, fresh sardines—these things were all new to me back then," Gilberg recalls.

Now Gilberg is the host. You'll find him in the restaurant's open kitchen, frying sardines and serving Portugal's staple salt cod four different ways. "Though in Portugal they say there's a different preparation of salt cod for every day of the week," the chef says.

Carne de Porco à Alentejana

"Pork and clams is on every Portuguese menu," says Koo Zee Doo chef-owner David Gilberg. "In this recipe, the flavors are true, but the one thing that makes it a little unique is that we braise the pork, which makes it more tender and flavorful. This dish is not spicy per se, but the piri piri at the end gives it an underlying hint of spiciness and brightens up the flavors."

(Note: *Massa de pimentão* must be made five days in advance. Pork must be marinated overnight.)

SERVES 4

For the massa de pimentão :

Kosher salt, as needed
3 large red bell peppers, seeded and
    cut into quarters

For the pork and clams:

1 head garlic, minced
2 bay leaves
2 tablespoons olive oil
1½ cups dry white wine, divided
2 pounds pork shoulder, trimmed and
    cut into 2-inch cubes
2 cups chicken stock
2 pounds littleneck clams or cockles
2 tablespoons kosher salt

For the potatoes:

4 cups canola oil
1 pound russet potatoes, peeled and
    cut into 1-inch cubes

For serving:

4 lemons, juiced
4 tablespoons cilantro, chopped
Piri piri or other hot sauce, as needed (available
    at Portuguese markets)

To prepare the massa de pimentão: Cover the bottom of a bowl with salt. Top with a layer of red peppers. Continue layering red peppers and salt, finishing with salt. Cover and refrigerate for 5 days.

Remove peppers from salt, shaking off excess salt. In a food processor, puree peppers until a paste forms.

To prepare the pork and clams: Mix garlic, massa de pimentão, bay leaves, olive oil, and ½ cup wine. Toss with pork to coat and marinate, refrigerated, overnight.

Preheat oven to 325°F.

In a deep, ovenproof saucepan over medium-high heat, sear pork cubes, working in batches if necessary. Remove pork and add remaining 1 cup wine to deglaze pan. Add chicken stock and bring to a simmer. Return pork to pan, cover, and cook in the oven for 1½ hours.

While pork cooks, rinse clams to remove grit and place in a large bowl of water with salt to clean. Refrigerate.

Remove pork from oven. Over medium heat, bring pork to a simmer. Rinse clams again. Add clams to pork and cover to steam clams open, 3 to 5 minutes.

To prepare the potatoes: In a large heavy-bottomed pan with canola oil over medium-high heat, fry cubed potatoes until golden brown, working in batches.

To serve: Add lemon juice, cilantro, and piri piri to pork and clams. Top with fried potatoes and serve.

STANDARD TAP

NORTHERN LIBERTIES
901 NORTH 2ND STREET
(215) 238-0630
WWW.STANDARDTAP.COM

Northern Liberties's Standard Tap was the city's first gastropub—before we even knew what that word meant and where exactly Northern Liberties was. The dimly lit bar, with a mix-tape-worthy jukebox and no televisions, with all local brews and a brusque chalkboard menu of smelts and duck confit, not nachos and potato skins, quickly became *the* standard.

"We wanted a place that was unpretentious, as easygoing as your favorite watering hole, that featured great local craft beer and uncompromisingly good food," says William Reed, who renovated and opened Standard Tap with Paul Kimport. "The renovations took three and a half years. That gave us a lot of time to hone in on exactly what we were building."

That was more than a dozen years ago.

Today the gastropub thrives in Philadelphia. (For a taste: Pub & Kitchen, page 102; N. 3rd, page 157; Good Dog Bar, page 124; and Resurrection Ale House, page 146.) And once-quiet Northern Liberties is now a nightlife destination. Standard Tap expanded, and then expanded again. But, thankfully, little has changed behind the bar, which now features twenty local taps, or in the kitchen, where chef Carolynn Angle works her magic on garlicky pulled pork sandwiches, luscious steak frites, and the justifiably famed chicken pot pie.

CHICKEN POT PIE

"This is like a really good chicken soup wrapped in puff pastry," says Standard Tap chef Carolynn Angle. The dish is so popular, it has been on the menu for more than ten years, but there's no special trick to making it at home. "It's all about letting the flavors develop slowly."
(Note: Chicken pot pie filling must be refrigerated overnight.)

SERVES 6

For the pot pie:

1 roasting chicken
1 cup kosher salt
16 cups cold water
Additional kosher salt and black pepper, as needed
Vegetable oil, as needed
4 cups crimini mushrooms, cut into quarters
1 tablespoon chopped garlic
3 cups diced celery
3 cups diced carrots
3 cups diced white onion
Chicken stock, as needed (see "Step by Step," page 131)
2 tablespoons chopped sage
1 cup unsalted butter, room temperature
1 cup quick-mixing flour
2 sheets puff pastry, defrosted

For the salad:

1 Granny Smith apple, peeled and chopped
1 large shallot, chopped
1 teaspoon chopped fresh thyme leaves
1 tablespoon chopped flat-leaf parsley
1 tablespoon Dijon mustard
1 cup apple cider vinegar
2 cups vegetable oil
Kosher salt and black pepper, as needed
1 head Bibb lettuce, chopped
¼ cup thinly sliced red onion
1 cup grape tomatoes

To prepare the pot pie: In a container large enough to contain water and chicken, combine salt and water. Submerge chicken and brine for 1 hour. Remove chicken, rinse, and pat dry. Season with salt and pepper.

Preheat oven to 350°F. Cover chicken with foil and cook until legs and wings pull easily from body, about 1 hour. Remove from oven and allow to cool. Once cool, pick meat from bones. (Reserve bones, skin, and fat if making stock.)

In a large saucepan over medium heat, heat vegetable oil. Add mushrooms and cook until caramelized. Add garlic and season with salt and pepper. Add celery, carrots, and onions and cook until just tender. Add chicken, season again with salt and pepper, and cook until all ingredients are heated through. Add chicken stock to cover. Bring to a boil and reduce to a simmer. Cook until liquid is dissolved by half. Add sage.

Using an electric mixer, whip butter until it has doubled in volume. Add flour and mix until fluffy.

Add butter-flour mixture to chicken mixture slowly, stirring until no flour is visible and mixture has a creamy appearance. Season with salt and pepper. Allow to cook completely. Refrigerate overnight.

Spray a large baking sheet with nonstick cooking spray. Cut each sheet of puff pastry into 6 even squares and place the squares on the baking sheet without touching. Add a heaping spoonful of chicken mixture into the middle of each square, piling mixture high, like a baseball. Stretch the remaining pastry squares over the mixture, bringing the edges of the top pastry to meet the edges of the bottom pastry. Press edges together tightly to seal and crimp corners. Refrigerate for 1 hour.

Preheat oven to 400°F. Bake until golden brown, about 30 minutes.

To prepare the salad: In a blender, combine apple, shallot, thyme, and parsley. Puree. Add mustard and apple cider vinegar and blend. While blending, slowly add oil to make vinaigrette. Season with salt and pepper. Toss ¼ cup of vinaigrette with lettuce, onion, and grape tomatoes. (Reserve remaining vinaigrette for another use.)

To serve: Serve chicken pot pies warm with salad.

STEP BY STEP: MAKING CHICKEN STOCK

"In a lot of dishes, stock is your flavor base. Your stock can make or break what you are doing," says Standard Tap chef Carolynn Angle. "The better your stock is, the better your end result will be." Angle's top stock-making tip: "Don't boil your stock too hard. It will get murky."

1. ROAST

Chop 1 white onion, 2 large carrots, and ½ head of celery. Coat lightly with vegetable oil and roast in a 400°F oven until vegetables caramelize.

2. SIMMER

In a large stock pot, combine bones and skin of a roasted chicken with 1 tablespoon black peppercorns, 4 bay leaves, 1 sprig thyme, and ½ cup parsley leaves. Add caramelized vegetables and cover ingredients with cold water. Bring stock to a boil, then reduce to a simmer. Simmer for at least 2 hours. The longer you simmer it, the more flavorful the stock will be.

3. SKIM

As the stock simmers, skim any fat that rises to the surface. When finished simmering, allow stock to rest, skimming off remaining fat. It is important to remove as much fat as possible.

4. STRAIN

Strain stock through a fine mesh strainer to remove remaining fat and solids.

5. STORE

This method will make about 1 gallon of stock. Stock can be refrigerated or frozen in convenient-size portions.

Pumpkin

Graduate Hospital
1713 South Street
(215) 545-4448
www.pumpkinphilly.com

Ian Moroney and Hillary Bor live in the city's Graduate Hospital neighborhood. So when the couple decided to open their first restaurant in 2004, they choose the just-south-of-Rittenhouse neighborhood, not despite its dearth of fashionable restaurants, but because of it. Pumpkin, a deli-turned-BYOB with butcher paper on the tables, was just what the neighborhood was craving. Moroney, no stranger to creating big flavors in a small kitchen from his years working with his father in the original Little Fish, served up rustic dishes of lamb shanks and short ribs and Provençal fish stew.

Moroney and Bor opened their second venture in Graduate Hospital, too (the now-shuttered Pumpkin Cafe). And their third, Pumpkin Market, also in Graduate Hospital, is a source of local produce, meats, and other artisanal products.

"We just wanted to make this neighborhood nicer," says Moroney.

In the years since Pumpkin opened, the rapidly gentrifying neighborhood has attracted residents and restaurants. And Moroney's cooking has changed along with the 'hood and the city's ever-growing restaurant scene. Refined has replaced rustic on the plate, though the dining experience remains neighborhood casual.

"I want the restaurant to thrive," says Moroney. "That means changing with the times and staying current and staying relevant."

One thing that isn't likely to go out of style: the line out the door for the restaurant's Sunday night prix fixe.

Stout-Braised Short Ribs with Maitake Mushrooms

"This dish started with the stout and the black garlic. We were just playing with those," says Pumpkin chef-owner Ian Moroney. The dish has a lot of steps, but don't let that intimidate you. "When you read a recipe—read it twice. Visualize it in your head. Literally picture every step," Moroney says, offering advice he follows. "Work slowly, work cleanly, and follow the method. It's not hard. It's not as hard as playing the guitar, anyway."

SERVES 4

For the short ribs:

4 short ribs, trimmed and tied by the butcher
Kosher salt and black pepper, as needed
½ cup bacon fat, divided
½ cup port
1/3 cup all-purpose flour
3 cups plus 2 tablespoons stout, divided

½ cup dried porcini mushrooms
4 sprigs thyme
2 bay leaves
1 tablespoon molasses
1½ teaspoons kosher salt
4 shallots, diced
10 cloves black garlic or white garlic

1 carrot, diced
1 rib celery, diced
4 cups beef stock
1 cup baby potatoes

For the mushrooms:

1 clove garlic, chopped
½ teaspoon kosher salt
¼ cup chopped flat-leaf parsley
½ cup diced pancetta
1¼ pounds royal trumpet or crimini
    mushrooms, cut in half

For the parsley puree:

3 cups flat-leaf parsley leaves
½ cup vegetable stock
⅓ teaspoon granulated sugar
Kosher salt, as needed

To prepare the short ribs: Preheat oven to 300°F. Bring short ribs to room temperature and season with salt and pepper. In a large, ovenproof saucepan over high heat, melt ¼ cup bacon fat. Sear short ribs until heavily caramelized on all sides, about 15 minutes. Remove ribs from pan and discard fat. Reduce heat to medium and add port to deglaze the pan, scraping up any browned bits. Sprinkle in flour and cook, stirring, about 5 minutes. Gradually stir in 3 cups beer until mixture is smooth. Add porcini, thyme, bay leaves, molasses, and salt.

In a sauté pan over medium-high heat, melt remaining ¼ cup bacon fat. Add shallots, garlic, carrot, and celery and sauté until lightly browned, about 10 minutes.

Transfer vegetables and short ribs to ovenproof pan and add beef stock to cover. Trim a piece of parchment paper to the size of the pan and rest on meat. Cover pan and transfer to oven. Cook until meat is fork tender, about 3 hours. Add potatoes and cook for 15 minutes.

Remove meat and potatoes from pan. Allow sauce to cool until fat rises, about 10 minutes. Skim fat. Discard thyme sprigs and bay leaves. Add remaining 2 tablespoons beer and season with salt and pepper. Return short ribs to sauce and keep warm over low heat.

To prepare the mushrooms: Mash garlic with salt. Add parsley to garlic mixture and roughly chop. In a large sauté pan over medium-high heat, cook pancetta until fat renders. Add mushrooms and cook until brown, about 10 minutes. Remove from heat and toss with parsley mixture.

To prepare the parsley puree: Fill a large saucepan with heavily salted water. Bring to a boil over high heat. Cook parsley leaves for 7 minutes. Strain parsley and plunge into ice water until cold. In a blender combine parsley and vegetable stock. Puree. Add sugar and season with salt. Pass through a strainer.

To serve: Untie short ribs and divide among four plates. Top with cooking sauce, parsley puree, and mushrooms.

PAESANO'S PHILLY STYLE

Two locations: Northern Liberties and Italian Market
152 West Girard Avenue, (267) 886-9556
1017 South 9th Street, (215) 440-0317
WWW.PAESANOSPHILLYSTYLE.COM

To an Italian, the word *paesano* means "villager." To chef Peter McAndrews, the definition is far more delicious. Paesano was the name that he and a fellow cook gave to their favorite late-night sandwich, a burger topped, quite improbably, with pancetta and garlic aioli and Gorgonzola dolce and french fries and a chefly drizzle of thirty-year-old balsamic vinegar. "It got the name Paesano's because you had to split it," says McAndrews. "You had to share it with a friend." So, when McAndrews opened his first sandwich shop, a small lunch counter across Girard Avenue from his Modo Mio (page 97), to share his love of "in your face sandwiches" with the city, it was Paesano's Philly Style.

"Philly is a big sandwich town—cheesesteaks, roast pork, hoagies—but not a deep one," says McAndrews, who would indulge his sandwich addiction on shopping trips to the Italian Market. "The sandwiches I got were always good, but they weren't great. I would bring them home and fix them. I wanted a sandwich that made a statement."

These sandwiches certainly do, even in the sandwich-rich Italian Market where McAndrews opened a second location. There seems to be no debate that McAndrews makes the best roast pork in the city, the meltingly tender Arista, layered with long hots, and the best hoagie in the city, the Daddy Wad, stuffed with five types of Italian cured meats. But it's McAndrews's own creations that have the biggest fans. The Paesano burger was retired in favor of the Paesano sandwich, equally worthy of the name: beef brisket topped with horseradish mayo and roasted tomatoes and pepperincino and sharp provolone and a fried egg.

LASAGNA BOLOGNESE

"We had lasagna Bolognese on the menu at Modo Mio when we first opened. If we had some left over, I would fry it up, put an egg on top, and put it on leftover bread. We knew it was good," says Paesano's Philly Style chef-owner Peter McAndrews. "When Paesano's opened, it was a natural fit."

SERVES 10

For the Bolognese sauce:

½ cup extra-virgin olive oil
2 medium Spanish onions, diced
4 ribs celery, diced
2 carrots, diced
5 cloves garlic, diced
1 pound ground veal
1 pound ground pork
¼ pound pancetta, diced
¾ cup tomato paste
1 cup whole milk

1 cup red wine
1 teaspoon chopped rosemary
Kosher salt and black pepper, as needed

For the smoked mozzarella besciamella:

5 tablespoons unsalted butter
¼ cup all-purpose flour
3 cups whole milk
2 pounds shredded smoked mozzarella
2 tablespoons kosher salt
½ teaspoon grated nutmeg

For the lasagna:

1¼ pounds pasta dough (See "Step by Step," page 83)
All-purpose flour, as needed
8 quarts water
2 tablespoons kosher salt
2 tablespoons extra-virgin olive oil
3½ cups prepared Bolognese sauce
8 ounces grated Parmesan cheese
1½ cups prepared smoked mozzarella besciamella

For serving:

Canola oil, as needed
1 cup all-purpose flour
15 large eggs, 5 eggs lightly beaten and 10 eggs fried
1½ cups bread crumbs
10 Italian rolls
Chopped rosemary, as needed

Special equipment: Thermometer

To prepare the Bolognese sauce: Heat oil in a saucepan over medium heat. Add onions, celery, carrots, and garlic and cook until translucent, but not browned. Add veal, pork, and pancetta. Increase heat to high and brown meat, stirring constantly. Add tomato paste, milk, wine, and rosemary. Bring to a boil and then reduce heat to simmer. Simmer for 1½ hours. Season with salt and pepper.

To prepare the smoked mozzarella besciamella: Melt butter in a saucepan over medium heat. Add flour and stir until smooth. Cook, stirring, until golden brown, 6 to 7 minutes.

Add milk, stirring constantly. Bring mixture to just under a boil and then slowly add mozzarella, stirring until fully incorporated. Add salt and nutmeg and remove from heat. Allow to cool to room temperature.

To prepare the lasagna: Divide the pasta dough into 4 portions. Roll each through the thinnest setting on a pasta machine and lay rolled pasta on a lightly floured surface to dry for 10 minutes. Cut the pasta into 5-inch squares and cover with a damp kitchen towel.

In a large saucepan over high heat, bring water to a boil. Add salt to water. Set up an ice bath and add olive oil to ice bath. Drop pasta into boiling water and cook until tender, about 1 minute. Transfer to the ice bath to cool, then drain on kitchen towels, laying the pasta flat.

Preheat oven to 375°F.

Assemble the lasagna in a 9 x 12-inch pan. Spread a layer of Bolognese sauce in pan. Sprinkle with Parmesan. Add a layer of pasta and top with besciamella. Repeat until all ingredients are used, finishing with a layer of pasta topped with besciamella and Parmesan. Bake until edges are browned and sauces are bubbling, about 45 minutes. Allow to cool, refrigerated, for 3 hours.

To serve: Fill a large, heavy-bottomed pan half full with oil. Over medium-high heat, heat oil to 350°F.

Cut lasagna into 10 pieces. Dredge lasagna pieces in flour, shaking off excess. Dip each piece of lasagna in egg, then dredge in bread crumbs, shaking off excess. Working in batches, fry lasagna in oil until crispy and golden brown, about 2 minutes.

Place fried lasagna in rolls. Top with remaining prepared besciamella, remaining prepared Bolognese sauce, and an over-easy egg. Garnish with rosemary.

THE DANDELION

RITTENHOUSE SQUARE
124 SOUTH 18TH STREET
(215) 558-2500
WWW.THEDANDELIONPUB.COM

The most striking thing about The Dandelion, from restaurateur Stephen Starr, is this: You hardly notice it there at the corner of 18th and Sansom. From the outside, the place doesn't exude Starr's typical panache, just a sense of quiet permanence, exactly what you expect in a classic English pub.

Starr installed a proper British accent in the kitchen—London chef Robert Aikens (pictured right), with his proper British fish-and-chips recipe and his dedication to precise metric measurements (kindly converted for this book)—and some less-than-proper British decorations in the warren of rooms carved from two storefronts. (Read the tongue-in-cheek embroidery that fills the quaintest of the dining rooms.)

"The Dandelion was originally going to be a gastropub"—a solid, safe formula of creative bar food and craft beers that Philadelphia has enthusiastically embraced—"but we found this English chef and, well, no one has really done a true English pub," says Starr.

"We have many a tradition in England, and I wanted to make people feel as if they were there when they dined at The Dandelion," Aikens, who has found himself explaining black pudding (blood sausage—"It is quite delicious and definitely worth a try," Aikens says) and defending his classic fish-and-chips, now a top seller.

Among those imported traditions: bubble and squeak, warm pints of hand-pumped English bitters, and even bank holidays, when the kitchen turns out a traditional roast complete with Yorkshire pudding. (Also available on Sunday for those who can't name a bank holiday.)

Fish & Chips with Tartar Sauce

"This fish-and-chips recipe has been with me for years," says The Dandelion chef Robert Aikens. "I've tweaked it a bit. Generally when people make a fish batter, they do it with just flour and beer. I've put in cornstarch to make it a little crisper and baking soda to make it a little lighter. Make sure the dry ingredients are well sifted, and when you put it in the liquid, the batter should have a thick, thick, thick custard consistency."

SERVES 4

For the tartar sauce (makes about 5 cups):

4 large egg yolks
3 tablespoons Dijon mustard
3 tablespoons lemon juice
3 tablespoons white wine vinegar
1½ teaspoons kosher salt
¼ teaspoon black pepper
3 cups vegetable oil
6 tablespoons olive oil
½ cup gherkins, roughly chopped
½ cup capers, roughly chopped
½ cup finely chopped shallots
4 tablespoons chopped flat-leaf parsley

For the chips:

5 russet potatoes, peeled
8 cups vegetable oil
Sea salt, as needed

Special equipment: **Thermometer**

For the fish:

8 cups vegetable oil
1½ pounds cod, pin bones removed
Kosher salt and black pepper, as needed
3 cups plus 6 tablespoons cake flour
3 cups plus 6 tablespoons all-purpose flour
1 cup cornstarch
2½ tablespoons baking powder
2 tablespoons kosher salt

4½ teaspoons granulated sugar
3¾ cups beer

Special equipment: **Thermometer**

For serving:

1 lemon, cut into wedges

To prepare the tartar sauce: In a bowl, whisk together egg yolks, mustard, lemon juice, white wine vinegar, salt, and pepper. In a separate bowl, combine vegetable and olive oils. Slowly add oil to egg mixture, whisking constantly, to form mayonnaise. (Add a few drops of water if mayonnaise breaks.) Stir in gherkins, capers, and shallots. Add parsley just before serving.

To prepare the chips: Cut potatoes lengthwise in ½-inch-thick batons. Wash starch from potatoes with cold running water.

Bring a large saucepan of heavily salted water to a simmer. Simmer potatoes until they soften, but don't break at the edges, 10 to 12 minutes. Remove potatoes and allow to cool.

In a large, heavy-bottomed saucepan over medium-high heat, heat vegetable oil to 285°F. Add potatoes and cook until slightly colored and soft, about 5 minutes. Remove and drain on paper towels. Increase heat until oil reaches 355°F. Return potatoes to oil and fry until golden

brown, about 4 minutes. Remove, drain, and season with salt.

To prepare the fish: Heat oil to 350°F in a large, heavy-bottomed saucepan over medium-high heat.

Cut cod into 4 portions. Dry fish well with paper towels and season with salt and pepper.

In a bowl large enough to fit cod portions, whisk together dry ingredients. Add beer and immediately dip fish in batter to coat. Gently place fish in hot oil, holding fish with tongs for a few seconds so batter seals. Fry until golden brown, 5 to 6 minutes. Remove fish from fryer and drain on paper towels. Season with salt.

To serve: Serve fish with 1 cup tartar sauce, chips, and lemon wedges.

Sabrina's Café

Three locations: Italian Market, Fairmount, and University City
910 Christian Street, (215) 574-1599
1804 Callowhill Street, (215) 636-9061
227 North 34th Street, (215) 222-1022
www.sabrinascafe.com

There are, certainly, other places to eat brunch in Philadelphia. But you wouldn't know that from the line that forms outside Sabrina's Café around 9 a.m. each Saturday and Sunday—rain or shine, August or February.

There are three tactics among the quirky cafe's regulars to deal with the wait, which can easily stretch to ninety minutes: Call ahead; although there are no reservations, the host will add your name to the growing list and estimate the wait time. Eat on a Tuesday at 2 p.m.; in 2011 the cafe finally started serving brunch all day. Or just enjoy it. There's always a coffee urn set up on the sidewalk, turning the sidewalk into an alfresco coffee shop where neighbors catch up while waiting for a table.

They are waiting for a peek at chef Lance Silverman's ever-changing blackboard of brunch specials (french toast filled with cream cheese and pineapple, fried trout with cheddar grits and poached eggs, pancakes topped with—believe it or not—strawberry pound cake) and consistent favorites like the Barking Chihuahua, the ultimate in breakfast burritos.

Owner Robert DeAbreu didn't expect to become the king of brunch when he opened the original Sabrina's—named after his newborn daughter—in South Philly in 2001. (The official name of the second location, opened in 2007, is Sabrina's Café & Spencer's Too, to be fair to his younger son.) The former Italian bakery had most recently been a short-lived breakfast and lunch spot, and as DeAbreu recalls, "I figured, I'm up early in the morning anyway."

Smoked Salmon Eggs Benedict with Home Fries

"We change the brunch specials every two weeks. This is a favorite on the blackboard menu," says Sabrina's Café owner Robert DeAbreu. "It is a little different because the hollandaise has a little spice to it. Everything we do is like that. Everything we do has a little twist that makes it Sabrina's."

SERVES 4

For the hollandaise sauce:

8 large egg yolks
½ cup lemon juice
2 tablespoons hot sauce
3 tablespoons hot water
½ cup unsalted butter, melted
2 teaspoons kosher salt
2 teaspoons black pepper
1 teaspoon ground cayenne pepper
2 tablespoons chopped tarragon

For the home fries:

3 pounds red bliss potatoes
2 cups vegetable oil, divided
2 white onions, julienned
2 tablespoons chopped garlic
2 tablespoons kosher salt
2 tablespoons black pepper
Additional kosher salt and black pepper, as needed

For the poached eggs:

2 tablespoons white vinegar
8 large eggs

For the spinach:

2 tablespoons vegetable oil
2 pounds spinach leaves
1 teaspoon chopped garlic
Kosher salt and black pepper, as needed

For serving:

4 English muffins, toasted
½ pound smoked salmon

To prepare the hollandaise sauce: Fill a saucepan with water and bring to a boil over high heat. In a metal bowl, combine egg yolks, lemon juice, hot sauce, and hot water. Place bowl over saucepan without touching boiling water. Whisk egg mixture rapidly, until it thickens and begins to set. Remove bowl from heat. While whisking, add melted butter. The mixture should be thick enough to coat the back of a spoon. If hollandaise becomes too thick, add a small amount of water. Add salt, pepper, cayenne, and tarragon. Keep warm until use.

To prepare the home fries: Place potatoes in a large saucepan. Add water to cover. Over medium-high heat, cook potatoes until fork tender. While potatoes cook, in a sauté pan over medium-high heat, heat 1 cup oil. Add onions, garlic, salt, and pepper and cook until onions are light brown. Drain onions.

Drain potatoes and allow to cool for 5 to 10 minutes. Cut potatoes in 1-inch cubes. In a sauté pan over medium high heat, heat remaining 1 cup oil. Fry potatoes until golden brown. Drain and combine with onions. Season with salt and pepper.

To prepare the poached eggs: Add vinegar to a large saucepan of boiling water. Crack eggs into

water and poach eggs until set, about 4 minutes. (See "Step by Step," page 69.) Remove poached eggs from water with a slotted spoon.

To prepare the spinach: In a large sauté pan over medium-high heat, heat vegetable oil. Add spinach and garlic. Season with salt and pepper. Cook until spinach is wilted.

To serve: Divide English muffins between four plates. Place a poached egg on each English muffins. Top with spinach, smoked salmon, and hollandaise sauce. Serve with home fries.

Pumpkin Pancakes

"The inspiration for pumpkin pancakes came by accident," says Sabrina's Café chef Lance Silverman. "We had a can of pumpkin puree in the restaurant by accident, and we thought having another pancake option was a good idea. Always use a nonstick pan. A regular pan won't do the job."

SERVES 4–6

5 large eggs
8 cups milk
3 tablespoons pure vanilla extract
2½ cups pumpkin puree
2 cups brown sugar
1 cup granulated sugar
10 cups all-purpose flour
¼ cup baking powder
¼ cup baking soda
Pinch of kosher salt
2 tablespoons cinnamon
2 tablespoons ground allspice
2 tablespoons ground cloves
2 tablespoons pumpkin pie spice
1 tablespoon ground ginger

In a bowl, combine eggs, milk, vanilla, and pumpkin puree. In a separate bowl, combine all remaining ingredients. Add dry ingredients to wet ingredients, combining with a whisk until just combined. Batter will remain slightly lumpy.

Heat a nonstick pan over medium heat. Spoon ½ cup batter into the pan per pancake and cook until pancake starts to bubble around the edges, 30 to 45 seconds. Flip pancake and cook an additional 30 to 45 seconds. Repeat until batter is gone. Serve warm.

Bibou

ITALIAN MARKET
1009 SOUTH 8TH STREET
(215) 965-8290
WWW.BIBOUBYOB.COM

There used to be a vaunted French bistro in this tiny, unexpected space, slipped in between the Italian butchers and Mexican markets of 9th Street and the Vietnamese flavors of Washington Avenue. It was called Pif, and diners mourned its closing in 2007.

Now there is an even more celebrated French bistro—just thirty-two seats and a peekaboo kitchen—in the same small space, making an escargot and bone marrow statement in a neighborhood better known for ravioli, tacos al pastor, and pho. *Bienvenue a Bibou.*

Charlotte Camels (pictured at right) gracefully runs Bibou's simple peach-and-gray dining room, managing eager diners and a constantly ringing phone. In the small kitchen, her husband, Pierre (pictured at right), a Le Bec-Fin alum, turns out a menu of uncomplicated French dishes that remind diners not so much of the still-missed Pif as the ideal mom-and-pop bistro somewhere in France.

Camels's confident flavors—*foie gras-*stuffed pig foot, juniper-scented sweet breads, crisp-skinned roasted duck—are a favorite among the city's wine lovers, who tote trophy wines for joyful dinners at the unfussy BYOB and make standing weekly reservations for the tough-to-get tables. Well-known wine expert Robert Parker is a fan, writing that Bibou "might be the best French bistro in the entire country," and, perhaps an even greater compliment, opening more than a dozen cellared wines at one dinner. And the warm, welcoming restaurant has earned raves from local and national food critics, including a spot on *GQ*'s 10 Best New Restaurants of the Year and a Best New Restaurant nomination from the James Beard Foundation.

Roasted Duck with Potato Crique & Asparagus

"There is texture and color on this plate," says Bibou chef-owner Pierre Camels. "We use a beautiful, tender duck. The sauce is rich and smooth. The asparagus brings freshness and crispness. And I love potatoes."

SERVES 4

For the potato crique:

2 Yukon Gold potatoes, peeled and grated
Kosher salt and black pepper, as needed
4 tablespoons extra-virgin olive oil, divided
3 teaspoons unsalted butter, divided

For the asparagus:

1 pound asparagus
1 tablespoon unsalted butter
Kosher salt, as needed
1 shallot, chopped
Chopped parsley, as needed

For the duck:

4 duck breasts, skin on
2 shallots, sliced
2 sprigs thyme
1 teaspoon black peppercorns, crushed
1 cup red wine
1 cup veal demi-glace (available at gourmet stores)
1 tablespoon unsalted butter
Kosher salt and black pepper, as needed

To prepare the potato crique: Preheat oven to 350°F.

Season potatoes with salt and pepper. In a 4-inch cast-iron pan over medium-high heat, heat 1 tablespoon olive oil. When hot, add one-quarter of potatoes, pressing to extract as much moisture as possible. Cook 30 seconds. Add 3 ¼-teaspoon pieces of butter to top of potatoes.

Continue to cook until butter melts and potatoes start to brown. Flip potato and transfer to oven, cooking for 4 to 5 minutes.

Repeat with remaining ingredients.

To prepare the asparagus: Trim asparagus stems to remove the woody base. Cut asparagus tips, about 1½ inches long. Chop remaining asparagus.

In a sauté pan over medium heat, melt butter. Sauté asparagus tips for 2 minutes. Season with salt. Add chopped asparagus and shallots and continue cooking for 1 minute. Remove from heat and add parsley.

To prepare the duck: Sear duck breasts in a sauté pan over medium heat, skin side down, until crispy. Flip duck breast and cook 3 to 4 minutes. Remove duck breasts to a rack, skin side down. Discard all but 1 teaspoon duck fat from pan.

Using the same pan, over medium heat, sauté shallots until lightly browned. Add thyme and peppercorns. Cook for 2 minutes. Deglaze with wine and cook until wine reduces by one-third. Add demi-glace and bring to a simmer. Add butter. Strain sauce. Season with salt and pepper.

To serve: In a separate sauté pan, re-sear duck breast, skin side down, to crisp. Flip duck breast and reheat, if necessary. Slice duck breasts. Divide duck breast between four plates. Serve with potato crique and asparagus. Top with sauce.

RESURRECTION ALE HOUSE

GRADUATE HOSPITAL
2425 GRAYS FERRY AVENUE
(215) 735-2202
WWW.RESURRECTIONALEHOUSE.COM

Resurrection Ale House is all about the beer—twelve often-exotic draft options on the ever-changing chalkboard menu, one beer engine, a forty-plus bottle list, beer-geek bartenders, and the ideal glassware for every brew. How can a chef compete?

With homemade pickles and an over-the-top lamb burger, chicken-chorizo ragu and roasted maitake mushrooms topped with hazelnut bread crumbs, and mom's fried chicken, a dish so good *Bon Appétit* came calling, that's how.

Resurrection Ale House's owners, husband and wife Brendan Hartranft (pictured at left) and Leigh Maida, have some practice creating a friendly neighborhood taproom, where good beer and good food coexist at a good price; Hartranft opened Kensington's Memphis Taproom, and the couple own West Philly's Local 44.

And chef Joey Chmiko has the laid-back attitude of a chef who's survived some of the city's busiest and most demanding kitchens: "We buy the best ingredients we can afford and do as little as possible with them," the chef says of his menu, which veers from the Mediterranean to the Middle East to Asia and serves up satisfying vegetarian dishes without apology or meat substitutes.

The only question Chmiko asks himself when creating a new dish: "When I can actually sit down and eat, would I love to have this with a beer?"

Twice-Fried Chicken with Watermelon-Basil Salad & Pickled Watermelon Rind

"This is a version of my mother's chicken recipe. It was a popular item at the house in the summertime. All the windows open, chicken frying in the cast-iron skillet, that smell wafting through the air, there's nothing like it," says Resurrection Ale House chef Joey Chmiko. "The second fry is the key move to crispy chicken. Give it the most love right there."

(Note: Pickled watermelon rind must be refrigerated overnight.)

SERVES 4

For the pickled watermelon rind:

4 cups peeled, diced watermelon rind (Reserve watermelon flesh for watermelon salad.)
2 cups rice wine vinegar
2 cups water
1 tablespoon cardamom pods
1 tablespoon coriander seeds
1 cup granulated sugar
1 tablespoon kosher salt
1 vanilla bean, scraped

For the twice-fried chicken:

Vegetable shortening, as needed
4 cups buttermilk
¼ cup Sriracha or other hot sauce
3 cups all-purpose flour
1 cup cornmeal
¼ cup Lawry's or other seasoned salt
8 bone-in, skin-on chicken thighs
Sea salt, as needed

Special equipment: Thermometer

For the watermelon salad:

1 cup basil leaves
¼ cup extra-virgin olive oil
1 small seedless watermelon, flesh cut into ½-inch cubes
Kosher salt, as needed

For serving:

1 cup honey
2 tablespoons Sriracha or other hot sauce

To prepare the pickled watermelon rind: Place the rind in a large heatproof container. Combine remaining ingredients in a nonreactive saucepan. Over high heat, bring mixture to a boil. Pour hot pickling liquid over watermelon rind. Cover and let cool completely. Refrigerate overnight. (Pickles will keep, refrigerated, for 3 months.)

To prepare the twice-fried chicken: Preheat oven to 350°F. In a large cast-iron sauté pan or dutch oven over medium heat, melt enough vegetable shortening to have 1 inch of fat. Heat oil to 300°F. Use a thermometer to accurately measure temperature.

In a bowl, whisk together buttermilk and hot sauce. In a separate bowl, combine flour, cornmeal, and seasoned salt. Working in batches as needed, dip chicken in buttermilk mixture, drain excess, and dredge in flour mixture, pressing flour into chicken and ensuring it is completely coated. Place coated skin side down in hot oil. Adjust flame as necessary to maintain 300°F temperature. Cook without moving until edges begin to brown, 8 to 10 minutes. Flip chicken and cook without moving until browned, 8 to 10 minutes. Remove chicken to a wire rack on a

baking sheet. Repeat until all chicken has been fried. Discard oil. Place chicken in oven until cooked through, 12 to 15 minutes.

While chicken is in the oven, again melt enough shortening in the cast-iron sauté pan or Dutch oven to have 1 inch of fat. Heat oil to 350°F. Remove chicken from oven. Working in batches as needed, fry chicken skin side down until a nice, deep brown color forms. Flip chicken and brown bottom side. Remove and drain on paper towels. Season each thigh with a pinch of sea salt. Allow to cool to room temperature.

To prepare the watermelon salad: In a food processor, pulse basil leaves until finely chopped, scraping the sides of the bowl as needed. Toss leaves with olive oil. Toss watermelon with basil and season with salt.

To serve: Whisk together honey and hot sauce. Divide chicken between four plates. Drizzle chicken with honey sauce. Serve with watermelon-basil salad and pickled watermelon rind.

ROASTED MAITAKE MUSHROOM WITH CELERY ROOT PUREE & GLAZED CARROTS

"This dish is very representative of the fall season for me," says Resurrection Ale House chef Joey Chmiko. "Root vegetables and mushrooms cooked simply. It's very satisfying to eat on a cool day. I enjoy meat, but I don't eat much of it. This dish has that 'meat and potatoes' feel without the meat or the potatoes."

SERVES 4

For the celery root puree:

2 pounds celery root, peeled and diced
4 cups heavy cream
½ cup water
1 tablespoon celery seed
2 tablespoons kosher salt
Additional kosher salt, as needed

For the mushrooms:

1 baguette, sliced ½-inch thick
3 tablespoons extra-virgin olive oil, divided
Kosher salt, as needed
1 cup hazelnuts, toasted
2 tablespoons finely chopped parsley
2 tablespoons sliced chives

2 pounds maitake mushrooms, bottoms trimmed (portobello mushrooms, stemmed and trimmed, may be substituted)
2 tablespoons unsalted butter
2 cloves garlic, skin on, crushed
2 sprigs thyme
Sea salt, as needed

For the carrots:

2 tablespoons extra-virgin olive oil
1 pound carrots, sliced 1/8-inch thick
Kosher salt, as needed
1 tablespoon butter
2 tablespoons chopped chives

For the salad:

¼ cup lemon juice
¼ cup extra-virgin olive oil
Kosher salt, as needed
4 cups baby arugula

To prepare the celery root puree: In a saucepan over low heat, combine all the ingredients. Bring to a simmer and cook until celery root is fork tender, 10 to 15 minutes. Remove from heat and strain, reserving cooking liquid and celery root. In a food processor, puree celery root. While processing, slowly add some cooking liquid until puree has the consistency of soft mashed potatoes. Season with salt.

To prepare the mushrooms: Preheat oven to 350°F.

Toss baguette slices with 1 tablespoon olive oil. Season with salt. Toast until browned and crisped, 8 to 10 minutes. Remove and cool completely. In a food processor, combine toasted baguette slices and hazelnuts. Pulse until coarse crumbs form. Stir in parsley and chives.

Season mushrooms aggressively with salt. Over medium-high heat, heat a cast-iron pan until very hot but not smoking. Add remaining 2 tablespoons olive oil and mushrooms, top down. Do not crowd pan. (Work in batches if necessary.) Cook, without moving, until browned, 2 to 3 minutes. Flip mushrooms. Add butter, garlic, and thyme. As butter melts, baste mushrooms with liquid for 2 to 3 minutes. Move pan to oven for 5 minutes. Remove pan from oven and continue to baste an additional 2 to 3 minutes. Drain mushrooms on paper towels.

To prepare the carrots: Heat a large sauté pan over medium-high heat. Add olive oil and heat until it slides fluidly across pan. Working in batches, if necessary, add carrots in a single layer. Toss carrots in olive oil and season with salt. Sauté, adding small amounts of water as needed to keep about 2 tablespoons of liquid in the pan, until carrots are al dente, 3 to 5 minutes. Remove from heat and add butter, tossing to coat carrots and emulsify with liquid in pan. Add chives.

To prepare the salad: Combine lemon juice and olive oil, whisking or shaking in a closed jar until emulsified. Season with salt. Toss with arugula.

To serve: Divide celery root puree between plates. Top with mushrooms sprinkled heavily with hazelnut bread crumbs and season with sea salt. Divide glazed carrots between plates and top with arugula salad.

GUAPOS TACOS

ROVING

WWW.GUAPOSTACOS.COM

Chef Jose Garces opened eight restaurants in five years. "Opening restaurants," he says lightly, "can be stressful." So, for the Iron Chef's ninth project: Guapos Tacos ("handsome tacos," in translation), a roving modern Mexican food truck glittering with 45,000 bottle caps, many collected from Garces's restaurants. "This," the chef says, "is fun."

Until the food truck trend heated up in New York and L.A. in recent years, Guapos Tacos would have seemed out of place in Garces's pantheon of restaurants. But he has always wanted to open a quick, causal taquería. Recalling his years of working the line at restaurants in New York, Garces says, "After work the only thing I could think of was having a cold beer and tacos. Now, I have my own taco truck."

Diners who love Garces's tortilla offerings at Distrito (page 10) were craving the same thing. Combining that hunger with the city's food truck trend allowed Garces to achieve another goal, too: "I wanted to bring the food we do to other parts of the city."

The truck has regular stops in Center City and West Philly, and, in the formula of the modern food truck, thousands of Twitter followers who seek out the truck whether it is at 20th and Pennsylvania or 43rd and Chester. (Plus, the truck doubles as a cool caterer for private parties.)

They are in search of tacos—green chile–chicken, chipotle short rib, duck barbacoa, carnitas—and the lines have been known to stretch one hundred deep during lunchtime stops at Love Park.

TACOS DE CARNITAS

"*Carnitas* is a real Mexican staple," says Guapos Tacos chef-owner Jose Garces. "When it is done right, it is a thing of beauty. The reheating process is really important. Get yourself a heavy cast-iron pan to crisp up the meat and then hit it with lime juice and cilantro."

SERVES 8

For the pineapple jícama salsa:

1 cup diced pineapple
1 cup diced jícama
½ cup diced red onion
¼ cup cilantro, chiffonade
1 serrano chile, thinly sliced
¼ cup honey
¼ cup pineapple juice
¼ cup extra-virgin olive oil
¼ cup lime juice
Granulated sugar, as needed
Kosher salt, as needed

For the carnitas:

6 pounds boneless pork shoulder
8¼ cups vegetable oil, divided
4 ounces pork lard
10 cloves garlic, crushed, plus
    4 tablespoons minced garlic
2 cups julienned Spanish onion
2 12-ounce cans evaporated milk
2 cups Mexican lager
1 cup fresh orange juice
2 navel oranges, cut in quarters
6 limes, cut in quarters
2 bay leaves
2 teaspoons black peppercorns
10 sprigs thyme
20 allspice berries
10 cloves
½ cup kosher salt
2 cups julienned red onion

½ cup thinly sliced cilantro
Lime juice, as needed
Kosher salt and black pepper, as needed

For serving:

Corn tortillas, as needed

To prepare the pineapple jícama salsa: Combine all ingredients for the salsa. Season with sugar and salt.

To prepare the carnitas: Preheat oven to 300°F. In a large roasting pan, combine pork, 8 cups vegetable oil, lard, 10 cloves garlic, Spanish onion, evaporated milk, lager, orange juice, oranges, limes, bay leaves, peppercorns, thyme, allspice, cloves, and salt. Cover pan with aluminum foil and cook until meat is tender, 3 hours.

Allow meat to rest in cooking liquid for 15 minutes. Carefully remove from pan. With your hands, gently shred meat into large pieces.

In a large cast-iron sauté pan over medium-high heat, heat remaining ¼ cup vegetable oil until just smoking. Add pork, remaining 4 tablespoons garlic, and red onion to pan. Cook until pork crisps. Carefully flip pork and add cilantro and lime juice. Season with salt and pepper.

To serve: Divide carnitas between corn tortillas. Top with salsa.

Perfect Pairing

THE COMMODORE
{VILLAGE WHISKEY}

"This is an approachable, easy-drinking cocktail," says bartender Keith Raimondi. *"It's a whiskey sour, basically, but the smokiness from the mezcal gives it an elevated feel."*

SERVES 1

For simple syrup (makes 1 cup):

1 cup granulated sugar
1 cup water

For the cocktail:

2 ounces Old Grand-Dad 100-proof bourbon
½ ounce lime juice
½ ounce simple syrup (recipe follows)
2 dashes Angostura Orange Bitters
Ice
1/8 ounce Los Nahuales mezcal
Orange peel garnish

Special equipment: Cocktail shaker

To prepare the simple syrup: In a small saucepan over low heat, combine sugar and water. Simmer until sugar dissolves. Allow to cool.

To prepare the cocktail: Combine bourbon, lime juice, simple syrup, and orange bitters in a cocktail shaker with ice and shake hard.

To a 14-ounce rocks glass, add mezcal and swirl to coat inside of glass completely. Leave excess mezcal at bottom of glass. Fill glass with ice and strain cocktail over ice. Garnish with orange peel.

118 South 20th Street
(215) 665-1088
www.villagewhiskey.com

A.KITCHEN

RITTENHOUSE SQUARE
135 SOUTH 18TH STREET
(215) 825-7030
WWW.AKITCHENPHILLY.COM

In the Philadelphia food world, the name David Fields is synonymous with Salt, his short-lived but influential Rittenhouse spot. The name Bryan Sikora is synonymous with Django, the landmark BYOB he ran with his then-wife, Aimee Olexy, near South Street, and Talula's Table, their Kennett Square chef's table, which earned the distinction of being the country's hardest reservation.

A.Kitchen, a collaboration between Fields and Sikora, is none of these things. It is, as Fields explains, "the way I want to eat now."

What Fields—and, judging from the lively dining room, Philadelphia diners—wants is a flexible dining experience. "I find myself more and more going out to places where I can eat however I want," says Fields. "I don't always want to have a traditional meal."

Sit at the bar or the open-kitchen counter, at a tucked-away banquette or a be-seen center table, or in the outdoor cafe (even in the rain!). Order wines—Field's passion, and the list reflects his taste for the distinctive and hard-to-find—by the three-ounce or five-ounce pour. And graze on Sikora's menu of what might be best called "medium plates." Not tapas, not entrees, these unfussy dishes—blue crab with farro and pesto, quail stuffed with Italian sausage and mushrooms, chicken risotto with corn broth—accommodate snacking, sharing, or a four-course meal.

"There's no theme here," says Fields. "This is not a trattoria. This is not a bistro. This is not an avant-garde, modernist restaurant. We want to break out of the formulas."

QUAIL STUFFED WITH ITALIAN SAUSAGE & MUSHROOMS

"Quail is a stunning presentation when stuffed," says A.Kitchen chef Bryan Sikora. "And people love sausage and mushrooms."

SERVES 4

¼ cup sliced shiitake mushrooms
¼ cup sliced maitake mushrooms
Olive oil, as needed
Kosher salt and black pepper, as needed
1 cup Italian sausage meat
2 tablespoons chopped shallots
3 hard-cooked eggs, chopped
1 teaspoon thyme leaves
2 teaspoons sliced parsley

2 cups cubed multigrain bread, toasted
4 semi-boneless quail
2 cups chicken stock
1 tablespoon vegetable oil
5 tablespoons unsalted butter
1 cup white beech mushrooms
1 leek, green part only, sliced into
    1-inch pieces

Preheat oven to 375°F. Toss shiitake and maitake mushrooms with olive oil to coat. Season with salt. Roast until mushrooms begin to steam, 5 to 10 minutes.

In a sauté pan over medium heat, cook sausage to brown and render fat, breaking up the sausage meat as it cooks. Drain rendered fat. Combine sausage meat with roasted mushrooms, shallots, eggs, thyme, parsley, and bread. Season with salt and pepper.

Season quail inside and outside with salt and pepper. Form a ball of stuffing large enough to fill the quail without tearing the skin. Stuff the quails and place them legs crossed and down on a plate and refrigerate 1 hour. Chilling will help keep the shape during cooking.

In a saucepan over medium-high heat, reduce chicken stock to ½ cup.

Preheat oven to 400°F.

Heat a sauté pan over medium-high heat. Coat with vegetable oil. Place quails in pan, legs down, and move pan to oven. Roast quail until lightly browned, about 15 minutes. Return pan to stove top over medium-high heat. Flip quail. Add butter and baste quail until browned and cooked through, about 2 minutes.

In a separate sauté pan over medium-high heat, sauté beech mushrooms and leeks in olive oil until leeks are translucent. Season with salt and pepper. Add reduced chicken stock and stir to combine and heat through.

To serve, spoon mushroom-leek mixture onto plates, add quail, and top with additional mushroom-leek mixture.

Lamb Loin with Treviso, Black Olives & Yogurt

"This dish is almost a salad," says A.Kitchen chef Bryan Sikora. "And it is certainly a summery dish with its Mediterranean flavors."

SERVES 4

1 cup oil-cured black olives, pitted, divided
¼ head roasted garlic
4 tablespoons olive oil, divided
4 5-ounce lamb loins
Kosher salt and black pepper, as needed
1 head Treviso radicchio
2 teaspoons lemon juice, divided
2 tablespoons unsalted butter
1 cup veal demi-glace (available at gourmet stores)
½ cup Greek yogurt

Chop ¾ cup olives and roasted garlic into small pieces. Combine with 1 tablespoon olive oil. Season lamb loins with salt and pepper. Lightly coat lamb loins with garlic-olive mixture.

Cut radicchio lengthwise into four pieces. Combine with 1 tablespoon olive oil and 1 teaspoon lemon juice. Season with salt and pepper.

In a sauté pan over medium heat, heat remaining 2 tablespoons olive oil. Add lamb loins. Cook for 5 minutes. Add butter and continue cooking, basting lamb loins with butter, for 5 minutes. Remove lamb loins. Discard excess fat from pan.

Using the same sauté pan over medium heat, place radicchio, cut side down, and sear until lightly browned. Remove radicchio. Reduce heat and add demi-glace and remaining ¼ cup black olives. Cook until heated through.

Divide yogurt between four plates. Add radicchio. Slice lamb and lay over radicchio. Top with demi-glace and olives.

N. 3RD

NORTHERN LIBERTIES
801 NORTH 3RD STREET
(215) 413-3666
WWW.NORTHTHIRD.COM

It's hard to know what to expect at N. 3rd. An oversized eagle-shaped kite hangs from the ceiling, and skulls and shamrocks share the walls. Pierogies, quesadillas, spring rolls, and steak frites share the menu. And diners and their dogs often share the dining room.

This is a beer bar with a surprisingly good under-$25 wine list and a neighborhood pub as frequently praised for its "N. 3rd's Famous" wings and other bar noshes as for its list of nightly bistro-style specials from the imagination of chef Peter Dunmire, a veteran of Rouge (page 60), Blue Angel, and some of Philadelphia's other top kitchens, who relishes the opportunity to cook simple food well at laid-back N. 3rd.

"I like to keep it simple. I know it doesn't sound exciting, but too few restaurants focus on preparing food right. As for myself, I want to be part of the revitalization of salt and pepper," says Dunmire, who was a regular at N. 3rd before becoming its chef.

Owner Mark Bee, plumber-turned-restaurateur, first moved to Northern Liberties in the 1980s. "There was nothing here," he says. When Bee, who would go on to revitalize Spring Garden's Silk City Diner, opened N. 3rd in 2001, there wasn't much more.

Now Northern Liberties is a hot spot, and N. 3rd is a de facto living room for this quirky corner of the neighborhood—a place to watch the Phillies game and to watch short films from Philly's amateur filmmakers during the popular Tuesday night "Fancypants Cinema" screening.

ASIAN-SPICED TUNA BURGER

"I was thinking about an option on the menu for people who wanted a burger but didn't want red meat," says N. 3rd chef Peter Dunmire. "We had an ahi tuna entree that was made from the eye of the tuna, and I thought I could fashion a burger from the trimmings. We put the sandwich on the menu, and it became so popular that we were soon using the entire tuna loin to prepare the burger."

Serves 4

For the tuna burger:

1½ pounds sushi-grade tuna trimmings
1 tablespoon finely chopped ginger
1 tablespoon chopped cilantro
1 tablespoon Sriracha or other hot sauce

1 teaspoon Dijon mustard
1 teaspoon toasted white sesame seeds
2 tablespoons vegetable oil

Special equipment: 4-inch ring mold

For the salad:

½ cup white miso paste
¼ cup mirin
1-inch piece ginger, peeled
1 naval orange, peel and pith removed
1 cup vegetable oil
2 cups spring mix greens

For serving:

½ cup mayonnaise
1 tablespoon wasabi paste
4 brioche hamburger buns, toasted

To prepare the tuna burger: Dice tuna. In a bowl, combine tuna, ginger, cilantro, hot sauce, mustard, and sesame seeds. Mix thoroughly by hand until well combined. Using a 4-inch ring mold, shape 4 patties, pressing tuna mixture together tightly.

In a nonstick sauté pan over medium heat, heat oil. Cook patties to rare, 1 minute on each side.

To prepare the salad: Combine miso paste, mirin, ginger, and orange in a blender. Blend until smooth. While blending, add vegetable oil to make dressing. Toss spring mix greens with 2 tablespoons of dressing. (Reserve remaining dressing for another use.)

To serve: In a bowl combine mayonnaise and wasabi paste. Spread wasabi mayonnaise on buns. Divide greens between buns. Place tuna burgers in buns.

BINDI

WASHINGTON SQUARE WEST

First came Lolita (page 184), Marcie Turney and Valerie Safran's marriage of Mexican and New American flavors. Then, in 2007, Turney and Safran moved across 13th Street and through hemispheres to create Indian-accented Bindi, a much-needed mid-range Indian restaurant in a city dominated by steam tables.

"In New York, there was Tabla and Tamarind," says Turney. "Philly didn't have that modern Indian-inspired cooking in a great atmosphere."

The couple followed Lolita's successful formula, a small, sexy cash-only BYOB that employs the flavors of a foreign land but pledges no allegiance to authenticity. Bindi's complex Indian spice mixtures—more than thirty blends are ground in-house—are simply a starting point. In Turney's kitchen, Indian standards undergo a Philadelphian update. Smoked salmon is cured in palm sugar, seasonal asparagus is dressed in curry and masala, and roasted duck is tucked into *pani puri*.

BINDI [2007–2011]

Unfortunately Bindi closed its doors in 2011.

WHY WE'LL MISS IT: "With Bindi I was hoping to bring a cuisine that is very misunderstood to the mainstream by using seasonal ingredients with traditional techniques—and do it in a modern, casual setting," says chef-owner Marcie Turney.

WHY IT CLOSED: "What we found is that people have a misconception of Indian food: 'It's all spicy,' 'I don't like curry,' 'I don't like Indian food'—I've heard it all," says Turney. "Bindi was before its time."

WHAT COMES NEXT: Turney and Safran's Spanish wine bar Jamonera is in the former Bindi space.

Chicken Tikka Kabob with Chickpea Curry

"Something spicy, something cooling, something sweet, something tangy, that's how we think about each dish," says Bindi chef-owner Marcie Turney. "The chicken tikka kabob has been on the menu since we opened. There's always someone in the group who is hesitant about Indian food, but everyone loves this dish. It is traditional but approachable. It's great in a wrap, too."

(Note: Chicken must marinate overnight. Fresh curry leaves and garam masala are available at Indian markets.)

SERVES 4

For the chickpea curry:

3 tablespoons olive oil
1 teaspoon cumin seeds
10 fresh curry leaves (optional)
¾ cup small-diced Spanish onion
1½ teaspoons kosher salt
½ teaspoon black pepper
½ tablespoon minced ginger
½ tablespoon minced garlic
½ teaspoon ground coriander
1/8 teaspoon turmeric
¼ teaspoon red pepper flakes
3 cups tomato puree
2 cups cooked chickpeas (if canned,
    rinse and drain)
1 cup chicken or vegetable broth
2 teaspoons garam masala
2 teaspoons lemon juice
2 tablespoons chopped cilantro leaves

For the raita:

1 cup plain yogurt
¼ cup diced cucumber, peeled and seeded
½ teaspoon minced jalapeño, seeded and deveined
¼ teaspoon toasted ground cumin
½ teaspoon lemon juice
1 teaspoon sliced cilantro leaves
1 teaspoon sliced mint leaves
¼ teaspoon kosher salt
Pinch of black pepper

For the kachumber:

¼ cup diced radish
¼ cup quartered baby tomatoes
¼ cup diced cucumber, peeled and seeded
2 scallions, sliced thin
2 teaspoons sliced cilantro leaves
1 teaspoon minced jalapeño, seeded and deveined
1 tablespoon lime juice
3 tablespoons olive oil
1/8 teaspoon kosher salt
Pinch of black pepper

For the chicken kabob:

¼ cup plain yogurt
1 lemon, juiced
3 tablespoons olive oil
½ tablespoon minced ginger
½ tablespoon minced garlic
½ tablespoon garam masala
1 teaspoon ground cumin
¼ teaspoon ground cayenne pepper
¼ teaspoon turmeric
1 teaspoon paprika
2 teaspoons kosher salt
4 6-ounce boneless, skinless chicken
    breasts, cut into 2-inch cubes

Special equipment: 8 wooden or metal skewers

To prepare the chickpea curry: Heat olive oil in a medium saucepan over medium-high heat. Add cumin seeds and curry leaves, if using, and cook until fragrant, about 20 seconds. Add onion, salt, and pepper and cook until onions begin to caramelize, about 4 to 5 minutes. Add ginger, garlic, coriander, turmeric, and red pepper flakes and cook another 30 seconds. Add tomato puree, chickpeas, and broth. Bring to a boil and then reduce heat to simmer for 15 minutes. Add garam masala, lemon juice, and cilantro.

To prepare the raita: In a small bowl, combine all ingredients and mix well.

To prepare the kachumber: In a small bowl, combine all ingredients and mix well.

To prepare the chicken kabobs: Combine all ingredients except chicken in a large bowl. Add chicken and toss well to evenly coat. Cover with plastic wrap and marinate, refrigerated, overnight. (If using wooden skewers, soak in water overnight.)

Remove chicken pieces from marinade and thread on skewers.

To bake skewers, preheat oven to 450°F. Place skewers in a baking dish at least 1-inch deep. Add 1 cup of water to pan. Roast until juice runs clear when chicken is pierced with a paring knife, about 10 to 12 minutes.

To grill skewers, preheat grill. Grill skewers until juice runs clear, about 4 minutes on each side.

To serve: Serve chicken tikka kabobs with chickpea curry, raita, and kachumber.

It has long been the favorite lament of the Philly foodie: *There's no good pizza in Philadelphia!* The city's restaurateurs—from Marc Vetri to Stephen Starr to Marcie Turney plus a few talented newcomers—heard the cry and answered with pizzas piled with spinach and goat cheese, pistachio and red onion, and pork and honey. For home cooks without a pricey custom-built pizza oven fueled by white oak, ash, and applewood to a searing nine hundred–plus degrees, the perfect restaurant pie may still be out of reach, but the city's top pizzaioli have some tips for the best at-home slice.

ZAVINO

Washington Square West
112 South 13th Street
(215) 732-2400
www.zavino.com

Pizzas aren't the only thing on the menu at this Italian addition to the city's newest Restaurant Row along 13th Street, but at the narrow restaurant's long bar, lively community and coveted sidewalk cafe tables, the char-rimmed pies are the number-one choice.

THE SECRET: "It is all about the dough," says Zavino chef Brent Hazelbaker. Zavino uses a Neapolitan-style dough. The dough is soft and silky and bakes up light and airy. "That is your foundation."

THE BEST SELLER: The Polpettini, starring miniature ricotta-stuffed veal meatballs. "We don't try to mask the pies," says Hazelbaker. "You need to use the right amount of toppings." The pizza has a base of crushed California tomatoes, topped with mozzarella, basil, shaved provolone, and those namesake meatballs.

TOP TIP: Heat it up. "You need to have the right temperature for the type of dough you are using," says Hazelbaker. Zavino's pliable dough is fired at 850°F, but a stiffer dough doesn't need quite as much heat—just a good pizza stone and practice transferring the pizza quickly and cleanly from a wooden peel into the hot oven.

BARBUZZO

Washington Square West
110 South 13th Street
(215) 546-9300
www.barbuzzo.com

When a small jar of oregano sprigs and another of Calabrian chili oil land on the table in crowded Barbuzzo, you know that your pizza will soon emerge from the open kitchen's dramatic wood-fired oven. The upscale answer to the ubiquitous shaker of red pepper flakes, these condiments promise a stylish, well-crafted pizza, and the kitchen delivers.

THE SECRET: The perfect "imperfect" pizza. "I have had many trainings with my line cooks on how to create the perfect 'imperfect' pizza," says Barbuzzo chef-owner Marcie Turney. "Pizza in Naples is not perfectly round, the crust has large charred bubbles, and the toppings are not heavy."

THE BEST SELLER: It's an every night competition between the simple Margherita (San Marzano tomatoes, mozzarella, basil) and the signature Ouvo (asparagus or brussels sprouts, depending on the season, guanciale, truffled egg, and "secret" white sauce).

TOP TIP: Keep it traditional. Barbuzzo pizza is pure Neapolitan. The dough is just flour, a little fresh yeast, and water. The sauce, raw San Marzanos and salt.

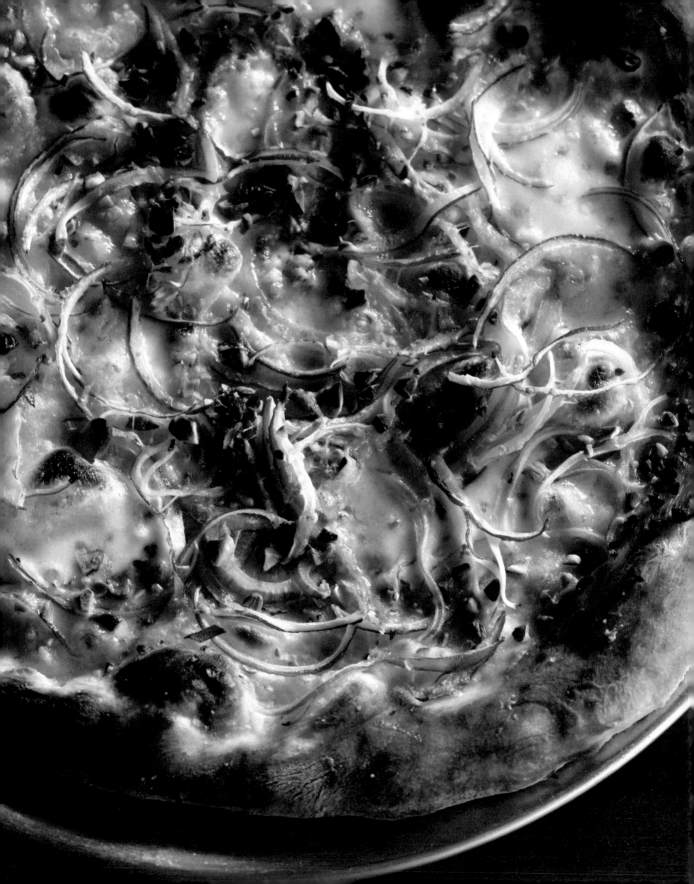

OSTERIA

North Philadelphia
640 North Broad Street
(215) 763-0920
www.osteriaphilly.com

Osteria was the first competitor in Philadelphia's delicious gourmet pizza wars, ending all *no-good-pizza!* complaints with thin, crisp-crusted pies topped with octopus and smoked mozzarella or pig trotters and peaches—or a simple Margherita that shines with San Marzanos, basil, and thick rounds of mozzarella.

THE SECRET: Balance. "The pizza needs all three components to be perfect," says chef-owner Jeff Michaud. "The crust has to be crispy and flavorful. The sauce has to taste fresh, and the ingredients you use have to be simple."

THE BEST SELLER: It's the Lombarda, topped with nutmeg-spiced cotechino sausage and a brilliant baked egg, versus the Parma, hidden under pale-pink prosciutto and piles of bright, peppery arugula.

TOP TIP: Take your time. "Make time to make it right," says Michaud. "You can't rush a good pizza dough."

PIZZERIA STELLA

Society Hill
420 South 2nd Street
(215) 320-8000
www.pizzeriastella.net

The pizza oven, stamped with the restaurant's name in red tile, is the center of attention at Stephen Starr's Stella, turning out hundreds of pies each night, each in under ninety seconds. When, shortly after the restaurant's opening, the beloved oven developed a crack, the restaurant was forced to close for several days, leaving the city without Stella's signature truffle pizza.

THE SECRET: "Definitely the dough," says Stella chef Shane Solomon, who blends several types of flour to get the restaurant's signature crust just right. The different flours allow Solomon to create a Neapolitan-inspired pizza with the firmer texture the American palate craves.

THE BEST SELLER: The Margherita and the dramatic Tartufo, layered with truffles in six different forms and topped with an egg, the bright yolk broken tableside. "It's something people probably can't get at their house," Solomon says. "It's luxurious."

TOP TIP: Practice. "It takes a lot of practice," says Solomon. "We make seven hundred pizzas a day, and we still aren't always happy with all of them."

KENNETT

Queen Village
848 South 2nd Street
(267) 687-1426
www.kennettrestaurant.com

The first idea was a pizza truck, with all locally sourced ingredients, so when the opportunity to open brick-and-mortar Kennett arose, chef Brian Ricci knew he wanted to serve up Neapolitan-style pies alongside lamb burgers and free-range chicken, roasted in the wood-fired pizza oven.

THE SECRET: The ingredients. Ricci uses high-gluten, organic Daisy Flour from Lancaster County, Jersey Fresh tomatoes ("Don't cook them!"), and Claudio's mozzarella. Plus, marjoram in place of oregano. "I don't think people use marjoram enough," he says.

THE BEST SELLER: The classic Margherita takes top honors, but the Porchetta gets honorable mention: slow-roasted pulled pork, house-made farmers' cheese, and local honey.

TOP TIP: "Get to know your oven," says Ricci. "Get your oven to the hottest temperature you can, but even then you are going to have hot spots. You are going to need to manipulate the pizza in the oven."

Desserts

This is a city with a sweet tooth. Water ice ranks with the pretzel and the cheesesteak for our caloric affection, and we lay claim to our own style of ice cream. Lancaster County is a bounty of produce, apple dumplings, and whoopee pies, and then there's the German butter cake, oozing rich, dairy sweetness.

We crave cheesecake (with Mexican caramel at Lolita, page 184, and with crème fraîche at Sbraga, page 179) and chocolate (in rich ganache form at Mica, page 183, and even richer fudge form at Betty's Speakeasy, page 175) after dinner, and carrot cake after breakfast—or perhaps *for* breakfast—at Honey's Sit 'n Eat (page 172).

For the eat-dessert-only crowd, there's city favorites Capogiro, which introduced Philly to Italian gelato in every flavor you can dream up, and Franklin Fountain, a re-creation of a classic soda fountain with, of course, Philadelphia-style ice cream. A fitting end to any meal.

FRANKLIN FOUNTAIN

OLD CITY
116 MARKET STREET
(215) 627-1899
WWW.FRANKLINFOUNTAIN.COM

In their pressed white button-downs, stiff white aprons, and proper black bow ties, the Berley brothers—Eric, with his handlebar mustache, and Ryan, sleekly Brylcreemed—look as though they stepped directly out of a sepia photograph and into the modern-day Philadelphia restaurant scene.

Franklin Fountain, their Old City soda fountain, revives the days more than a century past when Philadelphia was known far and wide for the superiority of its ice cream, made with high-quality dairy products of Lancaster County and without eggs. But despite its ancient marble counters and fountain, Franklin Fountain doesn't have a one hundred-year history; when the brothers first saw the space, it was a niche bakery called Eroticakes.

"We saw the long, narrow space, the great original character, the tin ceiling, and the penny tile floor and thought 'soda fountain,'" says Ryan Berley. And there was that impressive marble bar, now the soda fountain counter, in the basement of the antiques mall in Lancaster County where their mother is a dealer. So began their transformation from antiques dealer (Ryan) and philosophy student (Eric) to soda jerks, and later, as the Franklin Fountain expanded, classic candy makers. "Historically, that's what a lot of soda fountains did in the winter," says Ryan Berley.

History provided the decor, the recipes for floats, phosphates, and rickeys, and the name, borrowed from Benjamin, whose original print shop was across the street. "He started out on Market Street, too," says Ryan Berley. "He was walking the same pavement we're walking."

HOT FUDGE SUNDAE

"A classic hot fudge sundae was one of the things we had to have on the menu when we opened," says Franklin Fountain owner Ryan Berley. "Our hot fudge sundae has Philadelphia-style vanilla ice cream, which makes it a local specialty. In the late nineteenth century, Philadelphia ice cream was well known nationally as being the best, and we lay claim to creating vanilla with bean specks, which proved that it was real vanilla."

(Note: Ice cream base must be chilled at least three hours.)

MAKES 4 SUNDAES

For the ice cream:

1 vanilla bean
2 cups heavy cream
1 cup whole milk
1 cup granulated sugar
1¾ teaspoons Madagascar bourbon vanilla extract
¼ teaspoon Mexican vanilla extract

Special equipment: Ice cream maker

For the hot fudge (makes 5½ cups):

1⅛ cups granulated sugar
¼ cup light agave nectar
¼ cup water
½ cup unsalted butter
¾ cup whole milk
1¾ cups heavy cream
1 pound 60 percent cacao dark chocolate,
    broken into small pieces
1 pound 72 percent cacao dark chocolate,
    broken into small pieces

Special equipment: Thermometer

For serving:

Whipped cream (see "Step by Step," page 170)
4 maraschino cherries

To prepare the ice cream: Cut vanilla bean in half lengthwise and scrape out seeds. In a large saucepan over medium heat, combine cream, milk, sugar, vanilla bean seeds, and vanilla bean pod. Bring to a simmer.

Remove from heat and briskly whisk until sugar dissolves. Refrigerate mixture until very cold, at least 3 hours and up to overnight. Remove vanilla bean and discard. Stir in vanilla extracts.

Pour into an ice cream maker and process according to manufacturer's instructions. Serve immediately as a soft ice cream or freeze for a more solid treat.

To prepare the hot fudge: Bring sugar, agave, and water to a boil in a heavy-bottomed saucepan. Boil without stirring until mixture reaches 265°F. Add butter, milk, and cream. Whisk until butter is completely melted. Remove from heat and add chocolate, whisking continuously until fully incorporated. Serve immediately or refrigerate for later use. To reheat, warm small batches in the microwave for 30-second intervals, stirring, until thoroughly heated.

To serve: Line the bottom of four parfait glasses with a little hot fudge and add 2 or 3 scoops of ice cream to each glass. Top each with more hot fudge and garnish with whipped cream and a maraschino cherry.

STEP BY STEP: WHIPPING CREAM

"Whipping cream is ridiculously easy and incredibly tasty to do yourself," says Franklin Fountain's Sara May. "Those canned whip creams are pale imitations and are much more expensive."

1. CHILL

Start with a well-chilled metal bowl and well-chilled cream. A lower temperature will give more volume to your whipped cream.

2. COMBINE

When ready to whip, combine 2 cups heavy cream, 2 tablespoons granulated sugar, and ½ teaspoon pure vanilla extract in the chilled bowl.

3. WHIP

Using an electric mixer, or a whisk and some muscle, whip just until hard peaks form. Take care not to overwhip.

4. SERVE

Serve immediately with your favorite dessert.

HONEY'S SIT 'N EAT

NORTHERN LIBERTIES
800 NORTH 4TH STREET
(215) 925-1150
WWW.HONEYSSITNEAT.COM

This is the reason Jeb Woody and his wife, Ellen Mogell, opened Honey's Sit 'n Eat: Jeb's Open Faced Biscuit Sandwich, $6.50.

"I grew up in the South, and when I got up here, it was culture shock," says Woody. "I missed the simple things, the non-foodie aspect of going out." What Woody craved—what he ate every day at Honey's Sit 'n Eat long before it made the menu—was two fried eggs and two veggie sausages on a split biscuit smothered in cream gravy and, when Woody's eating, lots of Sriracha sauce. "Good ingredients and good food without paying for ego. That's why we opened this place."

Take Woody's Southern upbringing and add Mogell's Jewish one, plus Northern Liberties's come-as-you-are mentality and the Northeast's diner nostalgia, and you have the happy hodgepodge that is Honey's: hipster standing next to suburbanite in an hour-long brunch line, waiting for bagels and biscuits, *enfrijoladas,* tofu scramble, tuna melts, and a slice of one of those triple-decker cakes sitting on the lunch counter beneath diner-style domes.

The menu is, Woody says, "stuff we wanted to eat, the way we wanted to eat it," and the rustic, homey decor of the high-ceilinged space is a mix of salvage shop finds and pieces taken from Woody and Mogell's living room. "We like old stuff," Woody says, "and we wanted a place that looked like it had been there for a long time, a place that locals have been going to forever."

Carrot-Pecan Cake
with Maple–Cream Cheese Icing

"Our desserts are all the work of my wife and partner, Ellen Mogell," says Honey's Sit 'n Eat owner Jeb Woody. "One day she just decided we should have desserts. We sell a ton of them. We can hardly keep enough baked to keep them around. When there is a piece of cake left, I like to add a piece of cake to a milkshake."

MAKES 1 CAKE

4½ cups granulated sugar
1½ cups dark brown sugar
3 cups vegetable oil
11 large eggs
4½ cups flour
1½ tablespoons baking soda
½ tablespoon kosher salt
1 teaspoon cinnamon
1 teaspoon ground clove
Pinch of black pepper
6 cups (packed) grated carrots
2 cups chopped pecans
1-inch piece ginger, grated
½ teaspoon pure vanilla extract
1 pound cream cheese, softened
1 cup unsalted butter, softened
1½ cups confectioners' sugar
½ teaspoon maple extract
2 cups walnuts, toasted and crushed

Preheat oven to 325°F. Grease two 10-inch round cake pans.

In a large bowl, combine sugar, brown sugar, and oil. With an electric mixer, beat until smooth and thick. Add eggs one at a time, mixing until well combined. In a separate bowl, combine dry ingredients. Add dry ingredients to sugar mixture and mix until blended. Stir in carrots, pecans, ginger, and vanilla.

Divide batter between pans and bake for 50 to 60 minutes, rotating pans halfway through baking. Cool cakes in pans for 15 minutes, then transfer to racks to finish cooling.

Meanwhile, prepare maple–cream cheese icing. In a bowl, combine cream cheese, unsalted butter, confectioners' sugar, and maple extract. With an electric mixer, beat until fluffy.

Cut each cake in half horizontally. Stack layers, spreading icing between each layer and then frost cake with icing. Press walnuts into icing on sides of cake.

BETTY'S SPEAKEASY

Graduate Hospital
2241 Grays Ferry Avenue
(215) 735-9060
www.bettysfudge.com

Betty is owner Liz Begosh's grandmother, whose recipe for dark chocolate fudge with just a hint of peanut butter inspired Begosh's business. But Grandma Betty probably never imagined flavors like Blue Sue (dark chocolate fudge with the funky kick of local Birchrun Hills Farm blue cheese) and Victorious (milk chocolate with the crunch of cocoa nibs punched up with two types of local Victory beer).

Begosh first sold Betty's Tasty Buttons—made with fair-trade, organic, and local ingredients, packaged in brown paper boxes adorned with vintage buttons—at area farmers' markets. And it was the farmers she met there who inspired many of her fudge flavors and her next venture: Betty's Speakeasy, a cozy cafe and bakery, featuring local produce, usually in the form of fudge or Begosh's much-talked-about cupcakes.

"Betty's Speakeasy is meant to be a showcase of the best of what's coming out from local farmers and producers," says Begosh, surrounded by the evidence: strawberry preserves, blueberry pie bars, zucchini cupcakes. "Our brainstorming sessions are always fun. Our ideas are based on the season and what's going on in the producer world—or on what we're drinking and even what we're listening to."

The result: the cafe's outrageous maple pancake cupcake, topped with smoked sea salt buttercream, local bacon optional, inspired by a White Stripes song.

Squash Blossom Cupcakes

"A lot of people were asking for a pumpkin cupcake, but we had a huge amount of butternut squash coming in. We wanted to use that and make the pumpkin cupcake contingent happy," says Betty's Speakeasy owner Liz Begosh. "And the toasted pumpkin seed buttercream gives a really nice nuttiness. It almost tastes like buttered popcorn."

MAKES 16 CUPCAKES

For the cupcakes:

1 large butternut squash
¼ cup pumpkin ale (Betty's Speakeasy uses Weyerbacher Imperial Pumpkin Ale)
½ cup unsalted butter
½ cup light brown sugar
½ cup granulated sugar
2 large eggs
1 cup all-purpose flour
½ teaspoon baking soda
½ teaspoon baking powder
½ teaspoon kosher salt
½ teaspoon ground ginger
¼ teaspoon ground coriander
¼ teaspoon ground cardamom
Pinch of ground nutmeg
Pinch of ground clove

For the buttercream:

½ cup unsalted butter
3½ cups confectioners' sugar
4 teaspoons honey
4 teaspoons ground toasted pumpkin seeds
1–2 tablespoons heavy cream

To prepare the cupcakes: Preheat oven to 350°F. Roast squash until fork tender. Allow to cool. Peel and roughly chop. Puree in a food processor with ale.

Reduce oven heat to 325°F. Line a muffin pan with cupcake wrappers.

With an electric mixer, cream butter and sugars together. Add eggs one at a time, mixing to blend completely between each addition.

In a separate bowl, combine flour, baking soda, baking powder, salt, ginger, coriander, cardamom, nutmeg, and clove. Add to butter mixture in 2 batches, mixing to incorporate between batches. Add 1 cup roasted butternut squash puree and mix to incorporate. (Reserve remaining puree for another use.)

Divide batter between cupcake wrappers, filling three-quarters full. Bake for 24 minutes. Remove cupcakes from pan and allow to cool on a wire rack.

To prepare the buttercream: Cream together all ingredients .

To serve: Frost cupcakes with buttercream.

BETTY'S ORIGINAL FUDGE

"My grandmother Betty made fudge in her kitchen at Harvey's Lake for almost any occasion—holidays, birthdays, anytime we thought we really needed some creamy chocolate treat," says Betty's Speakeasy owner Liz Begosh. "She felt that to give someone a handmade treat was one way to show you cared."

MAKES ABOUT 80 SQUARES

½ cup goat milk
2 cups cane sugar
1 cup unsalted butter
3⅓ cups mini marshmallows
½ teaspoon pure vanilla extract
½ pound dark chocolate
2 tablespoons creamy peanut butter

Special equipment: Thermometer

In a large saucepan over medium heat, combine milk, sugar, and butter. Heat until mixture reaches soft-ball stage (235–245°F), 7 to 10 minutes. Remove from heat. Add marshmallows and vanilla. Stir until completely melted. Add chocolate and peanut butter. Stir until melted and thoroughly combined.

Pour mixture into a 9½ x 13-inch greased baking pan. Allow to cool completely. Cut into squares.

THE INGREDIENTS: WEYERBACHER BREWING COMPANY

In recent decades Philadelphia has become a bona fide craft beer destination. Exhibit number one: Beer Week, the country's largest beer festival, with ten days of beer tastings and brewer sightings. And the other fifty-one weeks a year, you'll see local suds flowing from tap handles that would, in other cities, be reserved for big national brands.

We still love our "lager" (that order brings a Yuengling, of course, our local brew before local was a compliment), but dozens of small breweries, like Weyerbacher in Easton, are changing how we think about—and drink—beer.

Thoughtful beer lists and beer-pairing dinners are a restaurant staple, and it only makes sense that the city's favorite brews would find their way into the kitchen and onto our dinner plates. Pale ale flavors the roast chicken at Pub & Kitchen (page 103), and stout braises the short ribs at Pumpkin (page 132). At Betty's Speakeasy, hearty Weyerbacher Imperial Pumpkin Ale is the key ingredient in cupcakes (page 174).

Weyerbacher, founded in 1995 in a livery by home brewer Dan Weirback, is one of the region's success stories, selling lager drinkers on unique, playful beers like Raspberry Imperial Stout, Belgian-style Merry Monks Ale, and even the signature malty and powerful Blithering Idiot Barleywine.

www.weyerbacher.com

Capogiro

Four locations: Washington Square West, Rittenhouse Square, South Philly, and University City
119 South 13th Street, (215) 351-0900
117 South 20th Street, (215) 636-9250
1625 East Passyunk Avenue, (215) 462-3790
3925 Walnut Street, (215) 222-0252
www.capogirogelato.com

You don't need to know any Italian to realize, just after that first bite of *cioccolato scuro* (deep dark chocolate) gelato or orange-cardamom sorbetto, that *capogiro* means "giddiness." Since Stephanie and John Reitano opened their first gelateria on 13th Street in 2002, the city—and everyone from Oprah to Rachael Ray—has been giddy over the small batch delights, made with local and seasonal ingredients in almost four hundred flavors. (About thirty are available each day, with an updated menu on their website.)

"In the beginning no one really knew what gelato was," says Stephanie Reitano. "They thought it was mousse. They weren't sure if it was pudding. Some people insisted it was ice cream. But once they saw it, they wanted to try it."

No surprise. The gelato is enticing, displayed as it would be in Italy, in wide, shallow containers topped with whole ingredients, and tasting is encouraged. Mixing and matching flavors—two to a small cup—is part of the fun. Reitano's favorite is *bacio* (chocolate-hazelnut) and hazelnut.

Capogiro, which was inspired by Stephanie Reitano's first taste of gelato during a 2001 trip to her husband's native Italy, now has four locations—and goes through more than one million brightly colored (and recyclable!) tasting spoons a year.

Strawberry-Absinthe Gelato

"Strawberry season in Philadelphia is exquisite," says Capogiro owner Stephanie Reitano. "At a dinner party, I clear the table and place my gelato mix into the ice cream machine while I warm a rustic tart, make the coffee, and put the grappa on the table. When the gelato is finished, we are ready to eat!"

(Note: Gelato base must be refrigerated overnight.)

SERVES 6

2½ cups whole milk
¼ cup coffee beans
1 vanilla bean, split
3½ x 2-inch piece lemon zest
3½ x 2-inch piece orange zest
5 large egg yolks

¾ cup plus 1 teaspoon granulated sugar, divided
1 pint fresh strawberries, hulled and quartered
2 tablespoons absinthe (Capogiro uses Philadelphia Distilling Co.'s Vieux Carré Absinthe Supérieure)

Special equipment: Ice cream maker

In a large saucepan over medium heat, bring milk to a simmer. Simmer for about 5 minutes. (Don't allow milk to boil.) Remove from heat and add coffee beans, vanilla, and lemon and orange zest. Cover pan with plastic wrap and allow milk to come to room temperature.

Remove plastic wrap and strain milk, reserving milk and discarding solids. Return milk to saucepan. Over medium heat, bring milk back to a simmer, never bringing to a boil.

While milk is reheating, combine egg yolks and ¾ cup sugar in a bowl. With an electric mixer, beat until mixture is thick and light yellow and has doubled in volume. Stop once to quickly scrape the sides of the bowl. With the mixer on medium-low, slowly add the warm milk in a steady stream. Mix completely, stopping once to scrape the

sides. Pour the mixture back into the saucepan and warm over medium heat, stirring constantly until mixture thickens and coats the back of the spoon, about 8 minutes.

Pour mixture into a large bowl and set in ice. Carefully stir the mixture to cool for about 5 minutes. Remove from ice and cover bowl. Allow gelato base to cool in the refrigerator overnight.

Toss strawberries in a bowl with remaining 1 teaspoon sugar. Allow to sit 20 minutes to soften. Process strawberries in a blender until smooth. Add strawberry puree and absinthe to gelato base and stir thoroughly. Pour into an ice cream maker and freeze according to the directions. Serve immediately. (Gelato will harden too much if stored in the freezer.)

THE INGREDIENTS: PHILADELPHIA DISTILLING CO.

Philadelphia Distilling Co., headquartered in Northeast Philly, has this claim to fame: It was the first craft distillery in Pennsylvania since Prohibition. And with its hand-hammered copper still, it kicked off a resurgence of craft liquors in the region. The company also has this claim to fame: Its high-quality liquors are a favorite of the best bartenders in town.

In 2006, the company debuted Bluecoat gin, a citrus-y answer to Christmas tree–scented brands. It seduced G&T drinkers and vodka martini types, who swore they didn't like gin. (Need to be convinced? Try Oyster House's Blanc & Blue Martini, page 58.)

The success of Bluecoat led to smooth, peppery Penn 1681 vodka, made with locally grown rye, and—after the federal government lifted the ban against it in 2007—Vieux Carré Absinthe Supérieure. When the herby anise liqueur premiered on New Year's Eve 2008, it was the first legal absinthe to be distilled on the East Coast in nearly one hundred years.

And it stoked the imagination of Capogiro's gelato makers, who turned the famously maddening drink into a sophisticated, strawberry dessert (page 176).

Next up from the spirits pioneers: XXX Shine, an unaged white whiskey that gets its name from its moonshine ancestors and its flavor from the state's corn harvest.

www.philadelphiadistilling.com

SBRAGA

AVENUE OF THE ARTS
440 SOUTH BROAD STREET
(215) 735-1913
WWW.SBRAGA.COM

Chef Kevin Sbraga's cooking is not authentic French. It is not authentic Italian. It is not authentic Mexican or authentic Malaysian.

"My food is never 'authentic,'" says the *Top Chef: Washington, D.C.* winner (pictured below). "My food is personal." That philosophy was a success in Singapore, where *Top Chef* held its season finale. Sbraga combined Southeast Asian ingredients and his personal approach to create a winning menu.

With the coveted *Top Chef* title, the prize money, and the recipe for his much-praised Singapore Sling panna cotta, Sbraga returned to Philadelphia to open his first restaurant, Sbraga, on the Avenue of the Arts.

Philadelphia foodies already knew New Jersey–born Sbraga for his time in the region's top kitchens, working for such restaurant bold-faced names as Georges Perrier, Stephen Starr, and Jose Garces. But for the chef—who grew up playing with flour in his parents' South Jersey bakery and has been working in the food industry since his first job at McDonald's at age fifteen—the dream has long been to open his own place, where he can cook his "personal" food, inspired by his Italian-American mother, his African-American father, his French-trained mentor, and his own experiences.

Now, he's cooking up an eclectic menu of eggplant terrine, grilled pigeon and beans, braised lamb with tamarind, and ricotta ravioli. The Singapore Sling is there, of course, alongside a menu of desserts created with one of Sbraga's culinary inspirations: his wife, Jesmary, an accomplished pastry chef.

Hazelnut & Black Cherry Cake with Yogurt Whipped Cream

"I'm inspired by two things: What I like to eat and what's in season," says Sbraga chef-owner Kevin Sbraga. "I created this in cherry season. There were cherries everywhere. And this cake is a favorite, especially the combination of hazelnuts and cherries."

SERVES 4

For the cakes:

¾ cup heavy cream
3 large egg yolks
1¼ cups granulated sugar
½ cup all-purpose flour
1⅓ cups hazelnut flour
1½ cups black cherries, pitted

Special equipment: 4 2½-inch tart pans

For the yogurt whipped cream:

½ cup heavy cream
3 tablespoons granulated sugar
½ teaspoon fine sea salt
½ vanilla bean, scraped
¼ cup plain yogurt

To prepare the cakes: Preheat oven to 375°F. Grease tart pans.

In a large bowl, whisk together cream and yolks. In a separate bowl, whisk together sugar and flours. Add flour mixture to egg mixture and stir to combine. Fold in cherries. Transfer batter to prepared pans. Bake until lightly browned and slightly puffed and no liquid is present, 7 to 8 minutes.

To prepare the yogurt whipped cream: Use an electric mixer to whip cream, sugar, salt, and vanilla bean scrapings until soft peaks form. Fold in yogurt.

To serve: Serve cakes warm with yogurt whipped cream.

CRÈME FRAÎCHE TART

"I grew up in my parents' bakery. We always had cheesecakes there," says Sbraga chef-owner Kevin Sbraga. "This tart is very similar to a cheesecake. Using crème fraîche instead of the traditional baker's cheese or cream cheese makes it lighter."

MAKES 1 6-INCH CAKE

1 cup blackberries
¾ cup granulated sugar, divided
2 limes, zested
1 cup vanilla wafer crumbs
¼ cup unsalted butter, melted
1 teaspoon fine sea salt
2 cups crème fraîche
2 large eggs
1 orange, zested
¼ cup heavy cream
½ teaspoon vanilla extract
½ cup all-purpose flour

Special equipment: **6-inch springform pan**

Preheat oven to 325°F. Grease springform pan.

Combine blackberries, ¼ cup sugar, and lime zest. Allow to sit for 1 hour.

Combine vanilla wafer crumbs, butter, and salt to form crust. Press into prepared pan, spreading evenly along the bottom.

Whisk crème fraîche, remaining ½ cup sugar, eggs, orange zest, heavy cream, and vanilla. Stir in flour until batter forms. Transfer to prepared pan. Place prepared pan in another pan filled with water. Bake until batter is just set, about 20 minutes. Allow to cool. Serve with blackberries.

PHILADELPHIA ICON: WATER ICE

Almost every city claims its own icy concoction. Philadelphians demand the delicate texture balance that is water ice, more liquid than a classic scrape-and-eat Italian ice, its nearest cousin, but not enough to turn the spoonable treat into a 7-Eleven Slurpee.

The alchemy is no easy task—a combination of water, sugar, fruit juice, and fruit pieces, stirred as it freezes to reach the exact neither-here-nor-there consistency.

Perhaps that's why the city's chefs tackle ice cream-, gelato-, and liquid nitrogen-anything, leaving the water ice to the old-school South Philly experts. If you see water ice on a Philadelphia restaurant menu, chances are it's mixed with vodka or rum, the only improvement that can be made on classic flavors from John's, Pop's, Mancuso's, Italiano's, or the undisputed queen of the scene, Rita's. The Bensalem-born franchise now boasts more than five hundred locations along the East Coast, which has done nothing to lessen the city's twenty-five-year love affair with Rita's water ice, served in those signature red, white, and green paper cups.

MICA

CHESTNUT HILL
8609 GERMANTOWN AVENUE
(267) 335-3912
WWW.MICARESTAURANT.COM

With Mica, chef Chip Roman (pictured below) is slowing things down. At BYOB Blackfish, Roman's first restaurant, tables turn over every ninety minutes, as expectant diners linger on the Conshohocken sidewalk awaiting their hour-and-a-half of bouillabaisse, five-spice lobster, and irresistible cinnamon beignets. At Mica, diners linger for two and a half hours over a ten-course tasting menu. "People aren't always used to the tasting menu approach," says Roman, "but it is a full experience of the restaurant." Plus, the chefs have more fun.

Ever since Roman opened Blackfish in 2007, suburb-wary Philadelphia diners have petitioned for a Roman restaurant in Center City. (Instead, Roman teased with two summer-only incarnations of Blackfish at the Shore.) With Mica's minimalist dining room in Chestnut Hill, he's come just a little closer, once again opening a bold restaurant—garlic-banana and black olive purees dress seared skate; chilled pea soup is decorated with wine-cured fish, dried and fried couscous, and citrus gel; even dessert gets the gelee-and-powder treatment—in a neighborhood without a strong restaurant reputation.

But Roman is reserved when describing Mica and its tasting menu experiment: "It's American food. Say 'American' and some people think hamburgers and hot dogs. But to us 'American' means there are no boundaries."

Chocolate Ganache with Raspberry Center

"Everybody loves a chocolate dessert," says Mica chef-owner Chip Roman. "We always have two on the menu, a plain one and a fancier one like this. But this is just a fancy chocolate mousse. It's still very approachable."

(Note: Chocolate ganache must be refrigerated overnight.)

SERVES 6

For the raspberry centers:

½ cup raspberry puree
¼ cup water
2 tablespoons tequila
½ cup granulated sugar

For the ganache:

2 cups heavy cream
5 sheets gelatin, bloomed
1¼ cups chopped dark chocolate
1 large egg yolk
½ teaspoon sea salt

Special equipment: 6 2 x 1½-inch metal cylindrical molds

For the coffee crumbs:

2 cups cake flour
6 tablespoons unsalted butter, room temperature
½ cup confectioners' sugar
1 large egg
1 teaspoon sea salt
3 tablespoons very finely ground espresso
¼ cup very strongly brewed espresso

For serving:

2 cups freeze-dried raspberries
Nut brittle (optional)

To prepare the raspberry centers: In a small saucepan over medium heat, combine all ingredients, stirring until sugar dissolves. Freeze in 2-teaspoon portions in an ice cube tray.

To prepare the ganache: Heat cream in a saucepan over medium heat. Remove from heat and add gelatin to dissolve. Place chocolate in a large bowl. Pour hot cream-gelatin mixture over chocolate, stirring until chocolate is fully incorporated. Whisk in egg yolk and season with salt.

Chill chocolate in refrigerator until thick but pourable. Prepare cylindrical molds by lining them with waxed paper well coated with nonstick cooking spray. Fill molds ¾ full with chocolate. Insert raspberry centers, using a toothpick to push them into the chocolate. Fill molds with remaining chocolate. Refrigerate overnight.

To prepare the coffee crumbs: Preheat oven to 350°F.

Using an electric mixer, combine flour and butter. Add sugar, egg, and salt and mix until combined. Add ground and brewed espresso and mix until loose dough forms. Chill dough, then roll dough ¼-inch thick on a parchment paper–lined baking sheet. Bake for 15 minutes. Allow to cool, then pulse in a food processor to form coarse crumbs.

To serve: In a food processor, process raspberries into a powder. Unmold chocolate ganache (warming molds gently will help release the ganache) and top with raspberry powder, coffee crumbs, and brittle, if using.

LOLITA

WASHINGTON SQUARE WEST
106 SOUTH 13TH STREET
(215) 546-7100
WWW.LOLITABYOB.COM

Philadelphia diners thought they knew Marcie Turney. She was the talent in the kitchen of Audrey Claire and Valanni, creating some of the city's favorite modern Mediterranean dishes. Then, in 2004, she opened her own restaurant—surprise!—Mexican-influenced Lolita.

"We love to eat Mexican food," says Turney, who owns the restaurant with her partner, Valerie Safran. "And every time we traveled to Chicago, we would make reservations at Rick Bayless's restaurants and think that there was no one doing anything like that here."

The instantly hip BYOB—or BYO tequila, the better to spike the restaurant's delicious margarita mixes—deftly combined Mexican flavors with New American dishes. The beet and goat cheeses salad was reimagined with mango, plantains, and a serrano-lime vinaigrette; cheesecake met cajeta caramel and the spice of ancho.

Turney and Safran, who also own the home store Open House, which opened on 13th Street a year and a half before Lolita, followed their popular Mexican restaurant with gourmet-to-go Grocery. Then came Indian-flavored Bindi (page 159, now shuttered), fashion and gourmet chocolate shop Verde and, finally, a return to Marcie's Mediterranean dishes with Barbuzzo (page 2) and Jamonera—all on the same block of 13th Street.

Turney says, "We just keep asking ourselves: What does this neighborhood need? What does every great neighborhood need?"

CHEESECAKE WITH CAJETA CARAMEL

"This recipe was a mistake," says Lolita chef-owner Marcie Turney. "This has been on the menu since we started, but we were making a much denser cheesecake. Then a cook mixed the cream cheese for too long, and it was so light that we kept doing it that way. The ancho chile in the chocolate cookie crumbles gives a little bit of heat. When they first saw that, people thought we were crazy."

MAKES 24 CUPCAKES

For the cajeta caramel:

1 cup heavy cream
½ teaspoon pure vanilla extract
½ teaspoon kosher salt
¼ cup unsalted butter

2 tablespoons light corn syrup
½ cup granulated sugar
½–1 tablespoon water
3 tablespoons young goat cheese

For the cupcakes:

1 cup ground dark chocolate wafers
   (Lolita uses Oreos)
⅛ teaspoon ground ancho chile
4 tablespoons unsalted butter, melted
1½ cups cream cheese, at room temperature
8 tablespoons granulated sugar, divided
1½ teaspoons pure vanilla extract, divided
2 large eggs
1 cup sour cream

For serving:

1½ cups toasted pecans
Whipped cream, as needed (see "Step by Step,"
   page 170)

To prepare the cajeta caramel: Combine cream, vanilla, and salt in a small saucepan over medium heat. Bring to a simmer. Add butter and remove from heat.

In a large saucepan, combine corn syrup and sugar. Add enough water to make the mixture look "sandy." Over medium heat bring sugar mixture to a boil, cooking without stirring and occasionally swirling the pan to mix. Cook until caramel is a deep amber color. Remove from heat and immediately add cream mixture. Be careful as it will steam and spit. Whisk to combine. Add goat cheese and whisk until smooth. Pour through a strainer.

To prepare the cupcakes: Preheat oven to 375°F. Line muffin pans with cupcake wrappers and spray inside of wrappers with nonstick spray.

In a small bowl, mix ground wafers, ancho chile powder, and butter until crumbs are evenly moistened. Place 1 tablespoon crust into each cupcake wrapper and pat down with the back of a spoon. Refrigerate 15 minutes.

In a large bowl use an electric mixer to beat the cream cheese until light and creamy, about 5 minutes. Add 6 tablespoons sugar and ½ teaspoon vanilla and beat until blended. Add eggs one at a time and beat until just smooth, scraping down the sides and bottom of the bowl so that all ingredients are thoroughly mixed.

Pour cream cheese mixture into cupcake wrappers, leaving one-quarter inch of space at top. Bake until cheesecake is firm, but not browned, and the center is set, 25 to 30 minutes. Remove from oven and cool for 30 minutes. (Cheesecake will fall slightly as it cools.)

In a small bowl, mix sour cream, remaining 2 tablespoons sugar, and remaining 1 teaspoon vanilla. Pour over cupcakes and bake 10 minutes. Transfer to rack to cool.

To serve: Serve cheesecakes at room temperature topped with cajeta caramel, toasted pecans, and whipped cream.

Perfect Pairing

DEATH RIDES A PALE HORSE
{THE FRANKLIN MORTGAGE & INVESTMENT CO.}

"Fino sherry is nutty, Aperol brings citrus, and bourbon brings spice," says bartender Colin Shearn. "Spice, nuts, and citrus is a classic combination, one that is found in a lot of desserts, too. This will pair well with them—or it can be enjoyed on its own as we serve it at the bar."

SERVES 1

For the demerare sugar syrup
    (makes about 1 cup):

2 cups demerara sugar
1 cup water

For the cocktail:

1½ ounces fino sherry
½ ounce Aperol
½ ounce Old Grand-Dad 114 proof bourbon
1 teaspoon demerara sugar syrup
    (recipe follows)
2 dashes orange bitters
1 dash absinthe
Ice

To prepare the demerare sugar syrup: In a small saucepan over low heat, combine sugar and water. Simmer until sugar dissolves. Allow to cool.

To prepare the cocktail: Stir all ingredients over ice until well chilled. Strain into a chilled cocktail glass.

112 South 18th Street
(215) 467-3277
www.thefranklinbar.com

Index

Acknowledgments

A final recipe. Yield: One beautiful cookbook.

For this recipe, I quickly discovered, the author's technique doesn't matter nearly as much as the quality of the ingredients:

Dozens of talented, passionate chefs and bartenders—and the restaurant owners and front-of-the-house and kitchen staffs supporting them—all of whom have been unfailingly generous with their time and their knowledge. It's a cliché to say I couldn't have written this book without them. It's also too small a sentiment: Without them, I *wouldn't* have written this book, because Philadelphia's dining scene wouldn't be the delicious phenomenon it is.

Clare Pelino of Pro Literary Consultants, who has the uncanny ability to assemble the right team for any cookbook.

The *Philadelphia Chef's Table* team: voracious photographer Jason Varney; the hard-working staff at Globe Pequot Press, specifically acquisitions editor Katie Benoit and development/project editor Tracee Williams; and fact-checker Nora Kelly.

The supportive directors and staff of The Food Trust, who, every day, broaden my understanding of how food can shape a community.

My fellow Philadelphia food writers, especially Rick Nichols and Ashley Primis, who graciously served as a sounding board throughout this project.

And my family and dearest friends—especially Vicki and her family, Michael and Aaron and, of course, Sasha—who have a talent for telling me just what I need to hear, whether that's "work harder" or "No more work. It's time for dinner."

About the Author

April White is an award-winning food writer and recipe developer. She is the author of several books, including *Latin Evolution,* the debut cookbook of Iron Chef Jose Garces. White is the former food editor of *Philadelphia* magazine, and her writing has also appeared in *Food & Wine, Every Day with Rachael Ray,* and *US Airways* magazine, among other publications. She lives in Philadelphia.